GAY
EUROPE

GAY
EUROPE

David Andrusia

A PERIGEE BOOK

A Perigee Book
Published by The Berkley Publishing Group
200 Madison Avenue
New York, NY 10016

Copyright © 1995 by David Andrusia

Book design by Rhea Braunstein

Cover design by James R. Harris

Cover illustration by Steven Salerno

First edition: April 1995

Published simultaneously in Canada

Library of Congress Cataloging-in-Publication Data

Andrusia, David.
Gay Europe / David Andrusia. — 1st ed.
p.   cm.
"A Perigee book."
ISBN 0-399-51910-6 (paper)
1. Europe—Guidebooks.   2. Gays—Travel—
Europe—Guidebooks.
I. Title.
D909.A55   1995
914.04'839—dc20   94-35102
                                     CIP

Printed in the United States of America

10   9   8   7   6   5   4   3   2   1

Contents

Contents

Acknowledgments

All my thanks go to:

> Katharine Sands, whose billboard sighting on Sheridan
> Square provided the brainstorm—hers!—for this
> book.
> Greg Ptacek, who thought of me to write it.
> Sarah Jane Freymann, head of Stepping Stone Literary
> Agency—mistress negotiator extraordinaire!

> . . . and, of course, Julie Merberg, my darling editor at
> Putnam, who believed in this book from the start.

In Transit

A book of this scope could not have been possible without
the kind—nay, enthusiastic!—participation of the fine airlines recognized here. They made *Gay Europe* a reality and
have my heartfelt thanks.

> AUSTRIAN AIRLINES offers flights between New York
> and Vienna nonstop, and from Chicago to Vienna
> via Copenhagen in conjunction with SAS.
> IBERIA, the national airline of Spain, operates nonstop
> flights from New York, Miami, Los Angeles, Mon-
> treal, and Toronto to Madrid, with connecting ser-
> vice to Barcelona, Ibiza, and all major cities in
> Spain.
> KLM ROYAL DUTCH AIRLINES offers nonstop service
> to Amsterdam from Atlanta, Boston, Chicago, De-
> troit, Houston, Los Angeles, Minneapolis/St. Paul,
> New York, Orlando, San Francisco, and Washing-

ton, D.C.; Canadians can fly nonstop from Montreal and Toronto, or from Ottawa (via Halifax) and Vancouver (via Calgary).

LUFTHANSA GERMAN AIRLINES provides nonstop service to Frankfurt—with direct service to cities in Germany and beyond—from Atlanta, Boston, Chicago, Dallas/Ft. Worth, Houston, Los Angeles, Miami, New York, Newark, and San Francisco. From Canada, fly nonstop to Frankfurt from Calgary, Edmonton, Ottawa, Toronto, and Vancouver.

SABENA flies nonstop to Brussels from the following American cities: Atlanta (in conjunction with their partner airline, Delta), Boston, Chicago, and New York.

TAP AIR PORTUGAL offers daily nonstop service to Lisbon, with connecting flights to other Portuguese cities and beyond—63 destinations in all—from Newark and New York.

VIRGIN ATLANTIC flies nonstop to London from Boston, Los Angeles, Miami, New York, Newark, Orlando, and San Francisco.

Very special thanks to:

LEADING HOTELS OF THE WORLD (Carol Poister and Karen Preston)
PRIMA HOTELS (Arjane van der Linden)

. . . and these organizations:

BELGIAN NATIONAL TOURIST OFFICE
BRITISH TOURIST AUTHORITY
FRENCH GOVERNMENT TOURIST OFFICE
SPANISH NATIONAL TOURIST OFFICE

Dear Reader:

At last! A gay travel guide that's reliable, contemporary, and totally up-to-date.

I know that's what you want, because I asked friends, acquaintances, and fellow gay travelers before writing word one.

And it's certainly what *I* wanted. As a travel writer for the gay and straight press, I spent countless wasted hours trying to find the best places to go in cities all over the world. (If you've ever used the other guides, you've experienced the same closed doors, non-existent addresses, and worthless cab rides as I have.)

But the wild goose chases end here! *Gay Europe* has everything you need to know, from clubs to restaurants to hotels . . . the best and brightest spots from Madrid to Milan. No more wasted hours and spoiled evenings—only gay old times and major fun.

I hope you enjoy reading this book as much as I enjoyed writing it. Most of all, I'd love to hear from you. Write to me c/o Perigee Books, The Berkley Publishing Group, 200 Madison Avenue, New York, NY 10016, and let me know what you liked, what you loathed, and any new discoveries you've found.

In the meantime . . . happy trails!

DAVID ANDRUSIA
New York City

Introduction

A couple of notes about the text are in order here.

Is this a gay place or not?

One of my main goals was to write a travel book for gays, not just a gay travel book. Of course, you'll find all of a city's important gay bars and clubs, but that's not all you want. (You might think it fun to visit gay restaurants where they exist, but you wouldn't want to neglect a city's other notable dining spots, would you?)

Thus, the following rule applies: hotels, restaurants, and cafés are not exclusively gay unless I specify them as such. With bars and clubs, the reverse is true; assume them to be gay except where I note that they're mixed. In either case, the descriptions for each entry should make an establishment's clientele clear to you.

How much does this cost?

Alas, the days when you could live in Europe for a year on $1,000—as recently as the '60s, according to legend—are long gone. So, too, are the bargains. This is primarily due to the urbanization and industrialization of postwar Europe and the dollar's comparative weakness to Continental currencies. (An exception to this rule is Portugal, which continues to be an inexpensive place to visit.)

Therefore, hotel prices vary surprisingly little from city to city: what's expensive in Paris is expensive in Rome. (When this differs, as in the case of Portugal, or in London—where budget hotels rarely show their faces—it is indicated in the appropriate chapter.) Also, rates vary widely from season to season, sometimes by as much as 75%; so use these price categories as a general guide.

That said, the following ranges apply (for double occupancy):

VERY EXPENSIVE	More than $220/night
EXPENSIVE	$175 to 220/night
MODERATE	$100 to 175/night
INEXPENSIVE	$75 to $100/night
VERY INEXPENSIVE	Less than $75/night

As for restaurants, I always note particularly expensive establishments and budget winners; where not noted, you can assume an eatery is moderately priced (usually between $15 and $25 per person, exclusive of drinks).

GAY
EUROPE

AUSTRIA

Vienna

Grand and homey, formal and friendly, welcoming yet mysterious, Vienna is a series of touristic contradictions. Could any other city have spawned Sigmund Freud?

To be sure, there's no mistaking that this is one of the great cities of the world. For centuries, of course, Vienna reigned supreme over Central Europe as the seat of the Austro-Hungarian empire. A political hub, certainly, but also a cultural capital nonpareil. Lovers of serious music have long made pilgrimages here, and no one with even a passing interest in architecture can ignore the city by the Danube. (Happily, most of the buildings damaged during World War II have been restored to their former majestic state.)

In contrast to the grandeur of the city's physique, the Viennese—at least, at first glance—seem friendly from a superficial point of view. *"Gruess Gott"* is the standard greeting of the day, and politesse is of huge importance here. Yet behind the gracious facade lies a near-tangible reserve that remains the hallmark of the Austrian soul. Neither "off-putting" nor "snobbish" is the operative word here; "reserved" is far more apropos. The country was under occupation for ten years after the war, and a feeling of insularity has continued to prevail.

In obvious contrast to, say, Spaniards, who are your best friends within five minutes of being introduced, Austrians—and especially the Viennese—are much harder to get to know.

Likewise, the social order in Austria is undeniably rigid. On the positive side, this results in a nation with a fraction of America's crime (excepting that which has occurred as a result of opening the borders to the former Eastern bloc refugees, who—after an initial bout with openheartedness—everyone wants to leave, posthaste). On the down side, this can also result in a repressed, fairly authoritative state, albeit one with one of the highest standards of living in the world.

Perhaps more than anything, Austria is in a state of flux: Its six million affluent, well-educated people stand poised to make theirs one of the most enviable democracies of the future, if a slightly monocultural and isolationist one. The living is good, even if diversity—and, to a lesser extent, personal freedom—suffers as a result.

This is nowhere more evident than in the lot of Viennese gays. Though a city of architectural and cultural greatness, Vienna is not the pop crossroads that London or Paris is, and a kind of sophisticated provincialism reigns. Unlike those other cities, Vienna does not embrace gays as a visible part of its societal landscape. Outside the confines of one's circle of friends, one doesn't flaunt one's sexuality—just as any unpleasantness is swept under the Viennese carpet without fail.

In a way, it's almost as if gays don't exist. Five years ago, there was a smattering of bars in the First District, the sought-after address within the first of Vienna's famous rings. Now the few gay places that exist have been banished to outlying districts. Why? According to one contact, a former *Interview* magazine staffer and the self-proclaimed biggest fag hag in Vienna, "The First is the 'elegant' district, showcasing the best of Austria, then and now. Gays aren't persecuted, but they're certainly not considered 'elegant,' and the city government would rather they not meet in the center of town." Whatever issues we face in America and Canada, one definitely is thankful for the relative freedom we enjoy in North America—and can only wonder at the psychological suffering of Austrian gays' "almost seen and never heard" veil.

Although exclusively gay bars no longer dot the streets of the prestigious First District, a diluted gay presence can still be felt. Gay men, especially alternative/bohemian types, do frequent the mixed bars noted below; though one could hardly call them cruisy, contact is possible, if not easy. In truth, you're far more likely to catch someone's eye wandering through the First, especially after dark, than pondering the suds in your beer at one of the "mixed" clientele bars.

But nobody goes to Vienna in search of the dizzying gay nightlife of New York or Madrid. You go to revel in one of the magnificent old cities of Europe, to stuff your face with Wiener schnitzel, and to sit in a café and watch the world go by. At least, that's reason enough for me—and I hope for you, too.

HOTELS

SACHER (Philharmonikerstrasse 4; 514560) One of the legendary hotels of the world, bar none. (Queen Elizabeth makes this her Viennese home—'nuff said?) You'll *know* you're in Vienna here! VERY EXPENSIVE.

BRISTOL (Kaertner Ring 1; 515160) Ultra-elegant yet surprisingly unstuffy hotel next to the Opera House. VERY EXPENSIVE.

IMPERIAL (Kaertner Ring 16; 501100) Very correct and Old Viennese place to stay, if the budget allows. VERY EXPENSIVE.

KOENIG VON UNGARN (Schulerstrasse 10; 515840) Fabulous old house turned wonderful new hotel. Just lovely! EXPENSIVE.

HOTEL ALTSTADT (Kirchengasse 41; 5263399) Vienna's premiere "boutique" hotel. Artsy, sometimes politico, crowd. Twenty-five rooms in old private house, with lovely common parlor. Highly recommended! MODERATE.

HOTEL ROEMISCHER KAISER WIEN (Annagasse 16; 512 77 510) Part of Best Western chain, but who'd know it? A charming slice of Old Vienna—and super-central, too. Recommended. MODERATE.

AUSTRIA (Wolfengasse 3; 515230) *Gemuetlich* little hotel that's calming and nice. A fine choice. MODERATE.

HOTEL ZIPSER (Langegasse 49; 4085266) Not the most central, but a good, quiet place at lower-than-expected prices. Very popular. MODERATE.

PENSION ACTION (Dorotheergasse 6; 5127949) The best value in the central ring. Old World charm for days, friendly/helpful staff. INEXPENSIVE.

PENSION WILD (Langegasse 1; 435174) Clean, popular pension near museums. Not gay, but attracts a queenly clientele of sorts. Basic, but fine. INEXPENSIVE.

RESTAURANTS

DO & CO (Stephansplatz 12, 6th floor)
Japanese/nouvelle menu in wonderfully panoramic setting. Downstairs: bar. Upstairs: upscale restaurant. Among Vienna's most chic.

DOMICIL (Rudolfsplatz 2)
Trendy nouvelle Austrian cuisine, fashionable crowd.

FISCHERBRAU (Bilrothstrasse 17)
Beer garden with wonderfully prepared classic Austrian food. Very authentic.

HEURIGER AM (Reisenbergerweg 1)
Austrian buffet—come hungry!—with great city view. Not trendy, but very Viennese.

KOENIGSBACHER BEI DER OPER (Walfischgasse 5)
Casual place that's great for Viennese specialties, at less-than-enormous prices. Nice!

KORSO (Mahlerstrasse 2, in the Bristol Hotel)
One of Austria's best. Gorgeous Art Nouveau style, top-of-the-line classic kitchen. A worthy splurge.

MAK (Stubenring 5, in Applied Arts Museum)
Ultra-trendy restaurant/café that's a scene day and night. Arguably, the hippest joint in town.

MOTTO (Schoenbrunnerstrasse 30)
Upscale "in" spot, home to Vienna's bold and beautiful.

OSWALD & KALB (Baeckerstrasse 14)
Bar/restaurant combo catering to an artsy crowd. A definite scene, best late-ish.

PLACHUTTA (Luegerplatz)
A restaurant of the moment, and a great place to sample the classic Austrian dish, *Tafelspitz*.

SACHER (Philharmonikerstrasse 4)
Nothing is more Old Vienna—the very quintessence of elegant Mitteleuropa. The Wiener schnit-

zel is fierce! (And who can visit Vienna without tasting a Sachertorte?)

SALZAMT (Ruprechtsplatz 1)
A must! Classic Viennese cooking in a fashionable—yet utterly unpretentious—setting. Moderate prices, too.

SCHLOSSGASSE 21 (Schlossgasse 21)
Big, beautiful garden, lovely in summer; Austrian and international specialties.

STEIRER ECK (Rasumofskygasse 2)
Ultra-elegant (jacket and tie, please) dining spot for that super-splurge or business date. The crème de la crème of Austria dines here.

TEMPEL (Zirkusgasse 52)
Very "in" restaurant featuring Austrian cooking in a traditional yet creative light.

TRZESNIEWSKI (Dorotheergasse 1)
An utterly unique concept: a sort of buffet/sandwich bar, full of Viennese specialties you won't see anywhere else. An institution you must "do" once.

VINISSIMO (Windmuehlgasse 20)
Upscale, chic wine bar with pastas and other light fare. See and be seen.

WILD (Neuemarkt 10–11)
Popular new designer restaurant; somewhat yuppie-ish, but worth the trip. Very "in."

CAFÉS

CAFÉ STEIN (Waehringerstrasse 6)
Modern café with upscale artsy crowd.

DEMEL (Kohlmarkt 14)
World-famous pastry shop chided by locals for their high prices. But again, an absolute must-do.

ENGLAENDER (Postgasse 2)
Part café, part restaurant, part bar, and totally trendy—Vienna's postpunk elite meet and greet in this exceptional rendezvous. An absolute must for the trendy gay.

FRAUENHUBER (Himmelpfortgasse 6)
Inspiringly classic Austrian Art Nouveau decor; pastries and java are tops.

HAWELKA (Dorotheergasse 6)
One of Vienna's grand cafés, attracting a semi-writerly crowd days and students/bohos/everybody else nights. Must be seen.

SLUKA (Rathausplatz 8)
The best sweets in town, say some; caters all the Austrian president's affairs.

SHOPPING

Vienna probably isn't top of mind for fashion mavens, but—surprise!—the city offers a tidy range of high-end haberdasheries and forward-looking shops, too.

The lion's share of shopping can be found in the First District, especially on Kohlmarkt, Graben, and Kärntnerstrasse, where elegant goods abound. More avant-garde clothing stores dot the Judenstrasse—here, the best are Front Line and Tomaso, but you'll find the places that most appeal to you. The underground mall at Karlsplatz conjures up more moderately priced stores (including Fiorucci), as well as a teeming drug and hustler trade. Less central is the Mariahilferstrasse, boasting a bevy of popularly priced wares. Hard-core shopping addicts may wish to trek out to SCS, the second-largest (but who's counting?) shopping mall in Europe, about ten miles from the city core. (Ask your hotel about public transportation possibilities.)

GAY

BARS

ALFI'S GOLDENER SPIEGEL (Linke Weinzelle 46)
Lots to eat—the home-cooked meals and the bar's hustlers both—in this admittedly curious Viennese institution. Worth a hoot, perhaps.

ALTE LAMPE (Heumuehlgasse 13)
Noisy old queens and highly Germanic singalong. If it's your bag . . .

BLUE BOY (Pressgasse 30)
New, all-purpose bar that looks to be a hit.

CAFÉ REINER (Kettenbruekengasse 4)
Very popular, fairly cruisy meeting spot, best from 10 P.M. on. A good place to size up the local scene.

EAGLE (Bluemelgasse 1)
Busy bar, ostensibly leather-oriented, but open to one and all.

MANGO BAR (Laimgrubengasse 3)
Probably Vienna's busiest bar; every imaginable kind of queer ends up here. You should, too.

NANU (Schleifmuehlgasse 11)
Decent bar with good-looking young crowd. Recommended.

SAVOY (Linke Weinzeile 36)
Mixed, but heavily gay, café that's especially attractive to the boho crowd. A must-do! (Open from late afternoon.)

MIXED BARS

Given Vienna's relative paucity of exclusively gay establishments, you may also want to know about the following mixed places. They should be of special interest to fashion victims and trendoids, less so to gay purists.

ALT WIEN (Baeckerstrasse 9)
Boho night crowd, very "in." A must for night-crawlers. Food, too.

BANE (Koelnerhoffgasse 3)
Cozy artists' hangout with wonderfully woodsy bar/café. Nice.

DANIEL MOSER (Rotenturmstrasse 14)
Fashion types, yuppies abound in this very "in" bar.

DIE BAR (Sonnenfelgasse 9)
Trendy modern bar with great tunes; gays, sometimes.

KRAH KRAH (Rabenstieg 8)
Loud, noisy bar that every visitor to Vienna should see. Slants young.

MYER'S AMERICAN BAR (Mayerhof 22)
Funky, forties-LA-style decor, very comfortable and cool. Cute bartenders!

STEINZEIT (Fischerstiege 9)
Vienna's most popular dive bar. Some gays.

DANCE CLUBS

U4 (Schoenbrunnerstrasse 222)
Thursdays only, from 11 P.M. on. The hippest light in the unglittering galaxy of Vienna's gay dance scene.

WHY NOT (Tiefer Graben 22)
Weekends only, Vienna's premier gay dance spot, if fairly standard issue for big-city queens.

SAUNAS

APOLLO (Wimbergergasse 34)
KAISERBRUENDL (Weihburggasse 18)
ROEMER (Passauer Platz 6)

BELGIUM

Brussels

Boring, banal, boorish ... poor Brussels has a rap sheet of blandness that's second to none.

Mais attention! Discount the Belgian capital's cadre of charms and you're throwing the baby out with the bathwater. And to lovers of food, art, and (sometimes) fabulous boys, that would be a big mistake.

Since the way to a man's heart is through his stomach, let's start with the food: Belgian cooking is enough to make a grown man swoon. Along with Lyon, it's the ne plus ultra of Gallic cuisine; yet *les chefs bruxellois* add touches that result in a national cuisine all its own. Partly responsible are the ingredients: seafood is key, and *moules-frites* (steamed mussels, often with garlic-butter sauce and to-die-for *frites*) is deservedly the national dish. (Don't miss those at Kelderke on the Grand' Place; they can't be beat!) But even classic French dishes are prepared with a distinctly regional flair, and the phrase "It's hard to get a bad meal here" is nowhere truer than in Brussels town.

In fact, before spending time in Belgium, I'd secretly mocked gastronomic tours (you know, the kind you see publicized in upscale travel magazines). So guess what—a weekend in Brussels is enough to make you fall in love with food all over again. (What—or whom—else you fall in love with is up to you.) Lovers of lettuce need not apply: This is the right stuff, from butter to béarnaise. Mention California Nouvelle and they'll laugh in your face. I'm not normally one to dictate an itinerary, but in this case I must: Miss Taverne du Passage, La Quincaillerie, and Bruneau at your own risk. Enough to warrant a sidetrip from Paris or Amsterdam? I vote a resounding yes!

Touristically, Brussels isn't a wellspring, but there's more than enough to keep you on the streets for a couple of days. Of greatest interest is the Old Masters Museum, especially if Brueghel is your bag. (An acquired taste, I know—how many Flemish peasants can the average man take?) A tour of the EEC headquarters area—each country is represented by typical eating places and bars—is also an afternoon's work. Café-hopping (anywhere they speak French, it's a national sport) and shopping (respectable, if not great) should round your trip out to a couple of days.

Brussels's gay life is about what you'd expect for a city of its size (approximately one million inhabitants)—nothing overly strenuous, yet more than enough to divert you during your stay. As in most European cities, the scene is concentrated in one main area (just off the Grand' Place) sure to be near your hotel. While you'll see your share of pasty Flems, the city's populace comprises primarily French-speaking Walloons, who (in my book) are far more lively and (certainly) *beau*. (For best results, try the Can-Can Taverne, Le Big Noise, or—on Sunday nights only—Le Garage disco.) There's also a gay restaurant, L'Annexe, that's dark and cozy, though hardly as gastronomically accomplished as the city's best joints.

For fabulous food and a classic Gallic (well, almost) joie de vivre, Brussels is an unheralded gem. Think about making it a part of your next Continental tour; you'll be glad you did.

HOTELS

AMIGO (1–3, rue de l'Amigo; 511 5910) Brussels's most charming address, a former prison turned upscale hotel, with fabulous results. A stone's thrown from the bars. EXPENSIVE.

METROPOLE (31, place de Brouckère; 217 2300) Nineteenth-century show palace; very Old World. A fine choice. EXPENSIVE.

PULLMAN ASTORIA (103, rue Royale 217 6290) Belle Epoque charmer with fabulous Pullman car bar. Nice! EXPENSIVE.

NOVOTEL (120, rue Marché-aux-Herbes 514 33 33) Right off the Grand' Place. Modern, somewhat antiseptic French chain hotel, but a good value and great location. MODERATE.

ARCHIMÈDE (22–24, rue Archimède; 231 90 90) Haven for groovy, artsy crowd. Highly recommended. MODERATE.

NEW HOTEL SIRU (1, place Rogier; 217 7580)
Uniquely designed hotel, where fashion types abound.
MODERATE.

LA LEGENDE (331, rue de l'Etuve; 512 8290) A good,
central budget choice. LOW MODERATE.

MOZART (15, rue Marché-aux-Fromages; 502 66 61)
Very central, unpretentious yet lovely budget choice.
INEXPENSIVE.

RESTAURANTS

AMADEUS (13, rue Veydt)
   Trendy eatery with slight Nouvelle slant. Upscale
   crowd; see-and-be-seen.

AU DUC D'ARENBERG (9, place du Petit-Sablon)
   Lovely, upscale townhouse restaurant full of dignitaries and such.

AU VIEUX ST-MARTIN (38, place du Grand Sablon)
   Casual, somewhat Bohemian crowd; good food at
   good prices. Very nice, very "in" spot.

BRUNEAU (73, avenue Broustin)
   Three-star marvel that's a must for serious gastronomes. *Menu de dégustation* a special must. COSTLY!

CHEZ JEAN (6, rue Chapeliers)
Fine Belgian food at user-friendly prices, in charming setting.

COMME CHEZ SOI (23, place Rouppe)
World famous, with Michelin-cited haute cuisine; one of Belgium's most sought-after restaurants. VERY EXPENSIVE!

KELDERKE (15 Grand' Place)
Always packed, a distinguished place to try the ever-popular *moules-frites*. Convivial and cute.

LA GRANDE PORTE (9, rue de Notre Seigneur)
Nightcrawlers love the retro ambience; good food, too. A definite scene.

LA QUINCAILLERIE (45, rue du Page)
An absolute must. Multileveled old hardware store, magnificent interpretations of classic fare. Much fun indeed.

LES ANNÉES FOLLES (17, rue Haute)
Classic yet informal Belgian bistro. Great food at less than monumental prices.

6E CONTINENT (88, rue Americaine)
Trendy new dining spot, across the way from the Quincaillerie in an upscale residential nabe. Looks to be a big hit.

TAVERNE DU PASSAGE (30, galerie de la Reine)
> Quite simply, my favorite place in town. Traditional cuisine and setting—a real Brussels find!

VINCENT (8, rue des Dominicains)
> Classic, casual bistro, friendly staff, fish is key. Not super-*cher*.

CAFÉS

A LA MORT SUBITE (7, rue Montagne aux Herbes-Potagères)
> No place says "Brussels" more. A huge, homey coffeehouse you can't afford to miss.

LE FALSTAFF (17–23, rue Henri Maus)
> Huge, rambling Art Nouveau café. Special.

LE SUE (35, rue de L'Éveiller)
> New watering hole for Brussels's would-be grunge crowd. I swear!

MOKAFE (9, galerie du Roi)
> Fabulous people-watching on the main pedestrian drag.

SNACK ARCADI (1 bis, rue d'Arenberg)
> Cute, cozy café with yummy sandwiches and international magazines. (Add massage, and I'm there for life!)

SHOPPING

Start at the gorgeous Galeries St.-Hubert, Europe's oldest urban arcade. This two-block stroll features an assortment of lovely shops, including a couple of great men's clothing stores and a to-die-for furniture mart. From there, walk down the nearby rue Neuve, rue Marché-aux-Herbes, and boulevard Anspach, home to a bevy of mid-range fashion stores. L'Innovation (111, rue Neuve) is a gallery-like department store, arguably Brussels's best.

More upscale is the avenue Louise and its surrounding arteries, especially boulevard Waterloo, where big names meet a few homegrown avant-garde designer types. Antiques queens will love the streets emanating from the Place du Grand Sablon (which offers an open-air market) on weekends.

GAY

BARS

CAN-CAN TAVERNE (55, rue des Pierres)
Busy, crowded, ultra-tiny bar—probably Brussels's best. Fabulous music, always!

HET RIJK DER ZINNEN (14, rue des Pierres)
Druggy, sleazy clientele, especially lively after hours.

L'ANNEXE (73, rue des Bouchers)
Aforementioned gay restaurant becomes a watering hole after about 11 P.M. Somewhat pissy crowd, to be sure.

LE BIG NOISE (44, rue Marché-au-Charbon)
Poppy, youngish bar. Worth a trip.

LE DUSQUESNOY (2, Dusquesnoy)
Leather bar.

LE SEPT (7, rue Platsteen)
Leather again.

DANCE CLUBS

CERCLE 52 (52, rue des Chartreux)
Popular disco cum backroom.

COU-COU (8, rue Jardin des Olives)
Elaborate Asian-Spanish drag queen shows. A semi-trashy hoot!

LE GARAGE (26, rue Duquesnoy)
Mixed, hip disco. Trendoids can go anytime, but recommended on Sunday, when clientele's all gay.

VAUDEVILLE (15, galerie de la Reine)
Mixed, fairly trendy crowd.

WHY NOT (7, rue des Riches-Claires)
   Small, exclusively gay disco with friendly staff. Best
   Saturday nights.

SAUNAS

Macho 2 (108, rue du Marché-au-Charbon)
Oasis (6, rue Van Orley)

DENMARK

Copenhagen

Lovely.

It's the first word that comes to mind in describing one of the most civil, charming, and cozy cities in the world. Simply everything about this friendly, gorgeous, happening place dares you *not* to fall in love.

After all, how can you fail to be seduced by a city where bus drivers are not only courteous, but act as unofficial tour guides as well, who, when thanked, reply "my pleasure" as you get off the bus?

Of course, it's not hard to be nice when you live in a city whose beauty practically knocks you over the head, where environmentalism is the order of the day and civic pride is ingrained at birth, and the history of a great city appears at every turn.

I'll avoid (well, almost) the obvious cliché of "Venice of the North," since Hamburg, Amsterdam, and other towns galore lay claim to the name. Yet Copenhagen's waterways are an integral part of the city's map, and as soon as you get out of the city center, bridges seem to be everywhere you look. As its names implies, Copenhagen is a haven, indeed.

Copenhageners seem constantly ready to apologize for their city's size—"We know this isn't Paris" is a cry often heard—but they hardly need to console. Warm, yes; embracing, certainly; yet Copenhagen hardly feels anything like a small town.

After all, who says a world-class city needs New York's skyscrapers or Paris's *grands boulevards?* Ubiquitous greenery and charming canals have a magnificence all their own. In Manhattan, everything seems a battle, an obstacle to a decent standard of life; Copenhagen, on the other hand, kisses you at every turn. In New York, bicyclists are a feared species; in this aggressively pro-environmentalist nation, bikes are an encouraged way to get around. And you rarely see those pretentious zillion-gear monstrosities; Denmark is flat, so old-fashioned bicycles (remember the kind the Wicked Witch of the West rode?) do just fine. And, my friends, there ain't much that's cuter than a Danish boy pedaling around town (except maybe the girls—both men and women in this country are extraordinarily good-looking).

On that note, I will diverge from my usual reticence and advise you that they don't call 'em Great Danes for nuthin'. (Details will be left to what I'm sure are your exceptionally vivid imaginations.) What's more, Danish boys are smart, curious about America, and usually very, very nice. (So sue me—even the most hard-boiled travel writer can fall in love.)

Not to stay fixated on size (ahem!), the visitor will be delighted to know that this city of one and a half million is rife with things to do. There are several excellent museums (the best is devoted to Danish art), world-renowned opera and dance (the Royal Danish has the cutest danseurs anywhere), and shopping that's second to none. Plus, there's a plethora of sensational cafés—something, to my mind, that no great city can be without.

By the way, if time permits, be sure to take a day-long tour of the castles in the Danish countryside. They're really worth seeing, and the lovely drive (several tour buses make the trip) is a treat unto itself.

Denmark boasts one of the highest standards of living in the world, a concerned citizenry, and a ruler, Queen Margarethe, who is universally adored (the country is the oldest continuous monarchy on Earth). Traveling to Copenhagen from New York, I felt as if I'd gone from a developing nation to the summit of the First World. And therein lies the city's only obstacle, and be forewarned: Copenhagen is one place you just won't want to leave.

HOTELS

HOTEL D'ANGLETERRE (Kongers Nytorv 34; 33 12 00 95) Copenhagen's grande dame and occasional home to dignitaries, kings, and queens. Lovely, spirited, and world-class. EXPENSIVE.

COPENHAGEN ADMIRAL (Toldbodgade 24; 45 33 11 82 82) Charming old Danish building alongside the harbor. Really special place. EXPENSIVE.

HOTEL PHOENIX (Bredgade 37; 33 95 95 00) First-class, yet unstuffy hotel just off the main drag. Lovely rooms, very helpful staff. HIGH MODERATE.

NYHAVN HOTEL (Nyhavn 71; 33 11 85 85) Charming and centrally located, recently renovated. An excellent choice. HIGH MODERATE.

NEPTUN HOTEL (Skt. Annae Plads 18; 33 13 89 00) Old World, uniquely decorated hotel right off the Stroget. HIGH MODERATE.

HOTEL WINDSOR (Frederiksborggade 30; 33 11 08 30) Heavily gay clientele, acceptable ambience. MODERATE.

WEBERS HOTEL (Vesterbrogade 11B; 31 31 14 32) A good budget choice in a city where cheap hotels don't come easy. INEXPENSIVE TO LOW MODERATE.

HOTEL SELANDIA (Hegolandsgade 12; 31 31 46 10) Perhaps the best really cheap hotel in town, though not super-central. INEXPENSIVE.

HOTEL JORGENSEN (Romersgade 11; 33 13 81 86) Excellent location; mixed, but gay-friendly, hotel. Café/bar on premises. INEXPENSIVE.

RESTAURANTS

Dining out in Copenhagen is not a cheap proposition, and most young Danes eat at home—this is not a city where cheap ethnic eateries abound. If you're not on business or feeling flush, there are a couple of alternatives: light meals in the aforementioned cafés,

or wonderful grilled wurst from one of the city's ubiquitous kiosks (don't turn up your nose—Copenhagen's
hot dog vendors are where rich and poor meet).

BARCELONA (Faelledvej 21)
Danish cooking belies the name; a hotspot among
Copenhagen's young, upscale crowd.

DOMHUSKOELDREN (Nytorv 5)
Danish food at popular prices, right in the middle
of town.

DOUBLE HAPPINESS (Gammel Kongejer 33B)
Cheap, good Chinese. If you're in the mood.

ERA ONA (Toregade 62)
Italian home cooking. Good food, in Copenhag-
en's only not-great neighborhood. Take a cab
home.

IDA DAVIDSEN (Skt. Kongensgade 70)
Great intro to Danish *smørrebrød* (delicious, gorgeously prepared open-faced sandwiches—often
fish—over buttered bread).

LA BRASSERIE (Kongens Nytorv 34)
Semi-trendy bar/restaurant in Hotel Angleterre. A
local scene of sorts.

NOUVELLE RESTAURANT (Gammel Strand 34)
Pricey, elegant Dutch/French cuisine, recognized
by Michelin.

PHILIPPE (Grabrodre Torr 2)
Most celebrated French restaurant in town; expensive, but worth it.

REEF 'N' BEEF (Landemaerket 27)
Australian cooking, with a young, somewhat gay crowd.

SLOTSKAELDEREN (Fortunstraede 4)
Well-known, cozy lunch spot frequented by Copenhagen's best. A wonderful way to experience *smørrebrød.* Recommended!

CAFÉS

Copenhagen's cafés are just what you think they are: cozy, clubby, and great respites from winter's cold (and, in summer, overflowing onto the streets). Unlike in New York, where faux-European cafés seem like geographical afterthoughts, Copenhagen's are part of the native scenery. Indeed, café-perching is as vital an element of daily life as the changing of the Royal Guard. Bring a book, park your butt, and do some serious people-watching at these happening spots:

CAFÉ DAN TURRELL (Store Regnegade 3–5)
Counterculturists abound. A tattered copy of anything by Genet helps achieve the right "look." Weekends, open late.

CAFÉ EUROPA (Amagertorv 1)

Right on the Stroget, the city's foremost shopping street. Not super-hip, but a good place to people-watch outside on warm days.

CAFÉ KRASNAPOLSKY (Vestergade 10)

A scene in which to be seen: high-tech decor, trendy crowd; good, cheap eats. Open till daybreak on weekends, thus the perfect post-club haunt.

CAFÉ SOMMERSKO (Kronprinsengade 6)

Upscale cool for Copenhagen's best and brightest. Worth one visit at least.

CAFÉ VICTOR (Nyostergade 8)

Haute-trendy crowd: bohos beware! The standard bearer for the city's bold and beautiful, and probably the costliest café in town.

SABINES CAFETERIA (Teglegaardsstraede 4)

Classic Bohemian haunt, *très* East Village; many arty gays come here. Open late.

SEBASTIAN (Hyskenstraede 10)

Every city should have one: a warm, bustling café where you can sit for hours and hours. Officially gay in the early evening, there is, in effect, a gay clientele all day long. Open till midnight, it's also a great alternative to the bars. I guarantee you'll spend many hours here!

ZELESTE (Store Strandstraede 6).

A lovely courtyard café is Zeleste's stock-in-trade. Cute, classically Danish decor. Pricey, but worth it.

SHOPPING

Even the most ardent anti-consumerist would be converted by Copenhagen, whose pedestrian-friendly center and gorgeously merchandised shops entice the most jaded retail eye. Practically all of the city's stores are on or near Stroget, Copenhagen's charming central promenade. Magasin (13 Kongens Nytorve) and Illum (52 Ostergade) are the major department stores; the former, especially, will remind you why we should rue the passing of grand old stores in America's downtowns. (Displays are neat and bright, the service staff as helpful as can be.) Like anyone who has ever visited Copenhagen, you'll scour the Stroget from end to end, and with good reason: This street contains Denmark's best shops, from local heroes like Georg Jensen and Matinique to trendy, international stores. You'll find your own favorites, so I'll not lead you by the neck here.

Devotees of the avant-garde will not want to miss Larsbjornsstraede and the tangential streets of Vestergade, Studestraede, and Sankt Peder Straede. Here you'll find clothes to rival the most outré of London or New York, as well as antiquarian booksellers, bitchin' hair salons, and the like. Flea market fans will have a heyday. Open from May through October, Copenhagen's are fab; you'll find them on Saturdays at Israels Plads, Frederiksberg, Norrebro, and the Forum. Shop wisely and well!

GAY

BARS

CAFÉ ADAGIO (Romersgade 11)
Connected to Hotel Jorgensen. Singers, sometimes. Just OK.

CAN-CAN (Mikkel Bryggers Gade 11)
Popular, upbeat drinking bar with mixed ages and types. Gets hot after midnight.

COSY BAR (Studiestraede 24)
Dark, popular watering hole with a fair smattering of boho types. After midnight, weekends best.

MEN'S BAR (Teglgardstraede 3)
Leather queens and wannabes.

DANCE CLUBS

AFTER DARK/METRO (Studiestraede 31)
Large dance complex cum backroom. Caveat emptor: "Membership" fees, entry, and drinks cost a small fortune. Still, this is Copenhagen's prime dance spot.

PAN DISCO (Knabrostraede 3)
    Legendary disco that threatens to close soon for "lack of funds," despite the pricey entry fee.

Saunas

COPENHAGEN GAY CENTER (Istedgade 36)
SAUNA CLUB AMIGO (Studiestraede 31A)

ENGLAND

London

"Here is London, giddy London/Is this home of the free or what?" asks Morrissey in "Hairdresser on Fire," his rollicking mantra to the English capital's dizzy social whirl.

The answer: not "or what"; London is as giddy and as groovy as it gets. While the UK continues to crumble—its economy and social programs pale in comparison to Europe's—London maintains a gorgeous, glossy veneer. No matter what happens in the rest of Britain, London remains one of the great cities of the world.

Forget the staid characters in a Barbara Pym novel; among the cadre of stylemakers, England swings. In fact, not since the sixties has the city been such a center of the fashion and nightlife worlds.

For starters, London now has—rejoice!—a happening restaurant scene. No, this ain't Rome or Paris (the indigenous cuisine is still ghastly), but there are enough foreign-trained chefs to populate a glittering gastronomic galaxy. "Nouvelle English" is the buzzword of the day, but it really incorporates the best of international cuisine. Ten years ago, fish and chips or Indian curries were the safest bets; today, a host of world-class restaurants abound.

The other good news is the gay scene—it's wild!

Time was, you were stuck with a smattering of boring bars in cloney Earl's Court; now you'll find pubs and clubs in every corner of London town. Soho is the newly sprung center of gay entertainment, boasting a bevy of Euro-style bars and—even better for the visitor with time on his hands—several *fagulous* cafés (see below). On nice days (admittedly, few to be had in Britain!), boys man the outside tables and watch the very hip world go by. These joints tend to be cliquey rather than cruisy, but hangin' out sans homeboys is just fine.

Remember that pubs close at 11 P.M., owing to restrictions legalized—I think—well before the U.S. was born. These anachronistic edicts are now relaxing somewhat, as some "modern" bars (and certainly the dance clubs) are permitted to stay open late (the tenuous distinctions among these are lost on me). Anyway, what this means is that, unless you're going out disco dancing (or, more appropriately, to an Ecstasy-saturated rave), strap on them cha cha heels early—not a bad idea for someone with sights to see the next day, *n'est-ce pas?*

On that note, London offers a range of touristic options like few other towns, from galleries to shows to the heady nightlife scene. But don't fail to ignore the biggest pleasure of all—aimless strolls around town. London is a series of labyrinthine lanes and unexpected green squares, and whilst on your journey, you're sure to find something—a park, a pub, a penis—to fall in love with on your own. After all, eating up the scenery is what a visit to London—or anywhere—is really all about.

HOTELS

First, a caveat: London hotels are very dear (that's expensive to you and me) in comparison to Europe's. You just ain't gonna find Paris's basic-but-fine two-star hotels or Italy's *pensione*. So if your budget is minimal, you may well want to consider one of the small gay hostelries, the Philbeach or the New York, which aren't super-central, but which offer good value for the price; or one of the other cheapies mentioned below. That said . . .

SAVOY (Strand; 836 4343) Incredibly grand landmark, impossibly luxurious and ve-ry British. The ne plus ultra of luxe. VERY EXPENSIVE.

DORCHESTER (Park Lane; 629 8888) London's other glittering star, home to the world's best and brightest. Expense accounts only, please. VERY EXPENSIVE.

CONNAUGHT (Carlos Place; 499 7070) Super-exclusive London residence; nothing is more correct or British. VERY EXPENSIVE.

BEAUFORT (33 Beauford Gardens; 584 5252) Old Victorian house turned hotel; excellent decor and Knightsbridge location. Charming. EXPENSIVE.

ABBEY COURT (20 Pembridge Gardens; 221 7518) Wonderful old Victorian house is now London's most well-known small hotel; exceptional furnishings. In funky Notting Hill Gate. EXPENSIVE.

SYDNEY HOUSE (9–11 Sydney Street; 376 7711) Absolutely lovely boutique hotel in a former private home. Exceptional staff, great Chelsea/South Kensington location. Perhaps the best value for the price in London. MODERATE.

PORTOBELLO (22 Stanley Gardens; 727 2777) Popular among artists, actors, etc., this boutique hotel in Notting Hill is a real find for the price. MODERATE.

WINDEMERE (142 Warrich Way; 834 5163) Basic but nice old hotel near Victoria Station, owned by a charming British couple. Excellent value. MODERATE.

ELIZABETH HOTEL (37 Eccleston Square; 828 6812) Modern and older parts coexist in this very central place; ask to see your room first. A good value. MODERATE.

JENKINS HOTEL (45 Cartwright Gardens; 387 2067) I know, I know: Whatever happened to Angela Cartwright? Anyway, this is a lovely old place in Bloomsburg. Off the beaten path but worth the detour. MODERATE.

PORTLAND BLOOMSBURY (7 Montague Street; 323 1717) Small, terribly lovely hotel near the British Museum. Quaint furnishings. Nice! MODERATE.

ASTER HOUSE (3 Summer Place; 581 5888) Fabulous, very central bed and breakfast, a blessing for the price (right in South Kensington). INEXPENSIVE.

EBURY COURT (26 Ebury Street; 730 8147) Nice small hotel, one of London's best bargains. Make sure your room has a private bathroom; not all do. INEXPENSIVE.

OBSERVATORY HOUSE (37 Hornton Street; 937 1577) Victorian bed and breakfast that's impossible to beat for the price; right in Kensington. INEXPENSIVE.

WINCHESTER (17 Belgravia Road; 828 2792) Simple yet acceptable B & B near Victoria Station. INEXPENSIVE.

GAY HOTELS

NEW YORK (32 Philbeach Gardens; 244 6884) Very popular gay hotel with all modern conveniences. Close to Underground and bars. MODERATE TO INEXPENSIVE.

NUMBER 7 (7 Josephine Avenue; 674 1880) Tiny gay guest house in semi-trendy Brixton. Close to the Fridge, if nothing else. INEXPENSIVE.

PHILBEACH HOTEL (30–1 Philbeach Gardens; 373 1244) London's oldest gay hotel—a legend. Helpful staff. MODERATE TO INEXPENSIVE. "Wilde About Oscar" French-y restaurant on premises.

RUSSELL LODGE (20 Little Russell Street; 430 2489)
Cozy li'l guest house in formerly literary Bloomsbury.
INEXPENSIVE.

RESTAURANTS

ALASTAIR LITTLE (49 Frith Street)
International-eclectic/Nouvelle menu in super-
modern setting, draws Soho's best and brightest
(more upscale than most). Recommended.

ALBERTO & GRANA (Chelsea Cloisters; 89 Sloane Avenue)
Trendy Spanish bar/restaurant, full of "Sloanies"
(formerly Sloane Rangers). Princess Di hangs
here.

ALL SAINTS (12 All Saints Road)
Notting Hill Gate's trendiest dining spot, devoted
to interesting interpretations of American regional
cuisine.

ARGYLE (316 Kings Road)
Modern English cooking with Far Eastern influ-
ences is the m.o. of this trendy Chelsea spot.

ATLANTIC BAR AND GRILL (Basement of Regent
Palace Hotel)
New trendspot with fabulous, simple preparations
of meat and fish. "In" plus.

BEACH BLANKET BABYLON (45 Ledbury Road)
Over-the-top, hyper-designed bar/restaurant with chic young crowd. Noisy.

BIBENDUM (81 Fulham Road)
Nothing less than London's hottest dining spot; Conran's most successful spot yet. Classic French dishes, perfectly done. Reservations a must.

BRIXTONIAN BACKYARD (4 Neal's Yard)
Caribbean eatery in working-class Brixton. The perfect pre-Fridge place to be.

BISTROT BRUNO (63 Frith Street)
One of London's best French restaurants, devoted to underutilized animal parts in inventive sauces. Pig's head is just the start. (I'm serious.) Very, very "in."

BISTROT 190 (190 Queensgate)
Southern European cooking is the draw here. Downstairs, there's a snacking menu that's less costly than upstairs.

CHRISTOPHER'S (18 Wellington Street)
American-updated cuisine, attracting politicos, actors, et al.

DELL'UGO (56 Frith Street)
Super-animated, way cool Mediterranean Soho restaurant. Groovy crowd.

FULHAM ROAD (259 Fulham Road)
   Famous Irish chef Stephen Ball holds court here.
   Upscale-trendy indeed.

GOPAL'S (12 Bateman Street)
   Arguably Soho's best Indian restaurant, a perennial favorite.

JULIE'S (135 Portland Road)
   Wonderful Notting Hill Gate place; a trendy wine
   bar cum classic English restaurant. Nice.

KENSINGTON PLACE (201 Kensington Church
Street)
   One of London's perennial "in" spots, packed for
   lunch and dinner both. A must.

LE PONT DE LA TOUR (Butler's Wharf)
   Excellent river view and fish-intensive menu make
   this a prime dining spot.

NOW & ZEN (44 Upper St. Martin's Land)
   Nouvelle-inspired Chinese/Japanese menu in minimalist design setting. Not cheap, but worth it. And
   so close to the bars!

QUAGLINO'S (16 Bury Street)
   Terence Conran's newest culinary crown. New
   English cuisine at its ultra-trendiest. Book far in
   advance!

SOHO SOHO (11–13 Frith Street)
>Downstairs: bar, light fare. Upstairs: full restaurant, bistro-style. Throngs of cool crowds; among Soho's best.

TATE GALLERY RESTAURANT (in the Tate Gallery, 'natch)
>French/international cooking—excellent!—in one of London's must-see galleries.

THE SQUARE (32 King Street)
>New temple of modern English cooking, tony crowd.

WAGAMAMA (4 Streatham Street)
>Communal Japanese eatery, packed to the gills. *Time Out* magazine award winner. A Young London scene.

ZOE (St. Christopher's Place)
>Haute-trendy, bi-level eatery owned by Antony Worrall Thompson, one of London's culinary stars. Upstairs: nouvelle café food. Downstairs: more substantial fare.

CAFÉS

KUDOS (10 Adelaide Street)
>Fun bar/café with light fare beginning at noon. Very nice indeed.

OLD COMPTON CAFÉ (34 Old Compton Street)
Super-trendy, always packed, especially the outside seats on a nice afternoon. A real London scene.

PATTISSERIE VALERIE (44 Old Compton Street)
Fabulous, funky boho café that's a Soho Institution.

SHOPPING

Dowdy dowagers and ring-nosed punkers, nothing in-between. That's many people's vision of the English fashion scene.

Now, the good news: Shopping in London is dizzy, dapper, and very diverse. Whether the Savoy or Soho is your stomping ground, you'll find everything you've dreamed of—and much, much more.

The energetic young'uns who work in London's stores are called shop assistants, not sales clerks. They're gaga for trends, are ultra-stylish, and super-nice—the obverse of sales help you find on these shores. In more cases than not, they'll put together an eye-turning outfit quicker than you can blink an eye, and help make shopping in London an experience you'll want to repeat again and again.

That said, here's a rundown on London's most important shopping nabes:

KINGS ROAD in Chelsea has faded somewhat from its Vivienne Westwood punk days—things are more mainstream today—but it's still an obligatory afternoon stroll.

KENSINGTON HIGH STREET abounds in pricey, trendy shops. Avant-garde designers show their wares in the mall-like Kensington Market and Hyper-Hyper, the two modespots fashion *victimes* will not want to miss. Kensington Church Street, which runs perpendicular, is also worth a look-see.

COVENT GARDEN is an urban mall full of informal eateries and shops. Even better are the boutiques on Neal Street, behind the center, and other surrounding arteries.

SOHO boasts an array of funky little stores that you'll doubtlessly stumble upon during your jaunts to the bars. Trendoid alert: Workers for Freedom (4 Lower John Street) is universally lauded as England's most happening design group.

OXFORD, REGENT, and BOND STREETS are probably London's best-known shopping strolls, and you'll want to "do" them briefly for touristic interest alone—but don't expect anything other than fairly conventional goods.

KNIGHTSBRIDGE offers high-end merchandise, English and foreign both. (Sloane Street is the main drag here.) This is also where you'll find the estimable Harrod's, arguably London's finest department store, though not of special interest to the fashion victim patrol.

OUTDOOR MARKETS are major fun. The best: Portobello Road on Saturday and Camden Market on Sunday.

GAY

CAFÉS

The recent emergence of London's fabulous gay cafés is a happy new addition to the scene. Don't fail to check their places out!

BALANS (60 Old Compton Street)
Absolutely trendulous café, popular all day long. So good even hetties come! Be prepared to whittle away hours. A must!

FREEDOM CAFÉ/BAR (60–66 Wardour Street)
Fabulous new gay café with unique drinks, sandwiches, and cakes. Busy from late afternoon on.

SILVER SCREEN CAFÉ (233 Earls Court Road)
Trendy bi-level gay bar/café with very friendly staff. A great place to linger on a rainy afternoon.

Bars and Pubs

Central

BASE (167 Drury Lane; nearest Underground (hereafter, "U"): Covent Garden)
Large, busy cruise bar with go-go boys and cute patrons. Check it out!

BOX (32 Monmouth Street; U: Covent Garden)
Busy new bar/café with cute young clientele. Looks to be a big hit.

BRIEF ENCOUNTER (42 St. Martin's Lane; U: Charing Cross)
Excellent after-work/early evening haunt that's always busy. A London landmark.

COMPTON'S (53 Old Compton Road; U: Leicester or Piccadilly)
Authentic English pub, fag style. Mixed bag, all ages welcome, from Soho trendies to older guys. Less important since the inception of the gay cafés on Compton St., but still worth a look-see.

CREW'S BAR (14 Upper St. Martin's Lane; U: Leicester or Piccadilly)
Huge Euro-style gay bar with many cute young things. Busy after 9 P.M.

EDGE (11 Soho Square; U: Tottenham Court Road)
Trendy bar/café in Soho attracts mixed crowd; a
great afternoon rest-your-feet stop-off.

KUDOS (10 Adelaide Street; U: Charing Cross)
Bi-level café/bar, with dinner specialties daily.
Upscale/chic decor and crowd.

LA RUE'S CAFÉ BAR (17 Manette Street; U: Tottenham)
Gay little bar/café that's open till 2 A.M. After-
pubbing crowd meets here.

LOCOMOTION (18 Bear Street; U: Leicester)
Trendy, young bar/café on Soho's edge. Good af-
ternoons.

PEACOCK (13 Maiden Lane; U: Charing Cross)
Popular piano bar catering to mature men and
show tune devotees.

PIANO BAR (8 Brewer Street; U: Leicester)
London's busiest, most well-established piano bar.

SUBSTATION (Falconberg Court: U: Tottenham)
Fagulous cruising basement bar that's open late
most nights (after pubs close). Hot! Hot! Hot!

VILLAGE SOHO (81 Wardour Street: U: Leicester or
Piccadilly)
Café by day, cruise bar from after-work on. Busy,
with cute young crowd.

79 CXR (79 Charing Cross Road; U: Leicester)
Open till 1 A.M.—a drawing card in London!—this new place boasts a quasi-Western motif and calls itself "an attitude-free zone." We'll see . . .

West

BROMPTON'S (294 Old Bridge Road; U: Earls Court)
Busy Earls Court bar that's full every night; geared toward seventies clone types more than trendies.

CHAMPION (1 Wellington Terrace at Bayswater Road: U: Notting Hill Gate)
Notting Hill's only gay venue, home to a mixed bag: everything from working-class types to punkers, with heavy emphasis on the former. Only if you're in the nabe.

COLEHERNE (261 Old Brompton Road; U: Earls Court)
A London institution; busy night after night. Mixed crowd, but definitely tends toward the leather/Levi's aesthetic. Perhaps London's oldest gay bar.

QUEEN'S HEAD (27 Tryon Street; U: Sloane Square)
Chelsea bar with hustler-y bent.

ROYAL OAK (62 Glenthorne Road; U: Hammersmith)
Sunday brunch for one pound! Traditional English pub; shows, sometimes.

South

ATTITUDE (The Trafalgar; 46 Sumner Road; U: Peckham)
> And how! Sleazy, dark bar with go-gos on weekends. Deliciously unEnglish!

MARKET TAVERN (Market Towers, 1 Nine Elms Lane; U: Vauxhall)
> Mixed bag disco. Monday and Wednesday, a leather crowd. Friday is the leather/fetishist party Saidie Maisie Club, hottest night in London for devotees of that scene.

ROYAL VAUXHALL TAVERN (1372 Kennington Lane; U: Vauxhall)
> Hip Sunday rave; other times, mixed gay/lesbian crowd in traditional English setting, usually with sing-along (loud).

East

WHITE SWAN (556 Commercial Road; U: Aldgate East)
> Working-class, local color East End crowd. Shows, sometimes.

North

BELL (257 Pentonville Road; U: King's Cross)
Bastion of London's alternative gay scene; mixed gay/lesbian crowd. A must for East Village types. Wednesday: Pop Tarts party, the best night to go.

CENTRAL STATION (37 Wharfdale Road; U: Kings Cross)
Cruise bar with theme parties; weekends tend to be trendier.

DANCE CLUBS

London's trendiest crowds follow a night-by-night plan to the Fabulous; as of this writing, the hippest gay nights are below. But be sure to check *Time Out*, London's wonderfully cool guide to what's happening, to know the latest goings-on (Yes, they do have a gay section!). Similarly, the gay rag *Fag Tag* will let you know what's what.

CAFÉ DE PARIS (3 Coventry Street)
Monday night attracts a hugely trendoid crowd. And you?

CIAO BABY (Town Hall Parade; U: Brixton)
London's hottest trendy gay night (formerly called The Daisy Chain). Not to be missed!

G.A.Y. (157 Charing Cross Road; U: Tottenham)
Saturday's dance madness, with equal smattering of mainstream and trendy gays.

HEAVEN (Under the Arches, Villiers Street)
World famous, huge seventies-style dance palace. Everybody and anybody.

PARADISE (Parkfield Street; U: Angel)
Super-steamy Sunday affair, on till 5 A.M. Very sexy!

QUEER NATION (4 the Piazza; U: Covent Garden)
Super-cool Sunday night dancefest.

SAUNAS

Saunas are illegal in the U.K.

Manchester

Grimy, gritty, and very groovy, Manchester is a city of today.

What else would you expect of the place that spawned Morrissey, New Order, and Lush? True, Manchester has no majestic monuments, magnificent museums, or paisley parks; and the weather's downright miserable. But as a center of England's music, arts, and fashion scene, it's really worth a look.

Don't get me wrong—I'm not advocating a fortnight's stay. However, the gateway to England's north, Scotland, and Wales can certainly merit a day out of anyone's British trip.

Manchesterians are duly proud of their city's place as the first industrial town in the world. The first railroad was built here, and the city remains the hub of the UK's apparel and textile trade. As a result, the city center is almost entirely commercial; unlike the citizens of most European metropolises, people here live out of town—imparting an odd, somewhat deserted feeling to the place after dark. But (past the obvious) Manchester is abuzz, full of cafés, bars, and restaurants to rival the Continent's best; and style permeates every facet of the city's social life (especially among gays and the young). The range of entries in each category below is proof positive of that!

There's only one word for Manchester's gay scene: remarkable. Not because you'll find the cornucopia of clubs and facilities of Paris, London, or New York—you won't—but because the gay population's immersion in all areas of municipal life is an undeniable force. Manchester's recent renaissance could not have been possible without gays' involvement in music, fashion, and the arts—and everyone knows it.

And, amazingly for what is in effect a provincial city, attitudes toward gays here are hearteningly tolerant, especially among the young. In most cases, being gay is very much a non-issue (if not an identity that carries outright cachet!). Too, Manchester is the largest university town in England—forty-five thousand students at the university and polytechnic—a fact that undeniably impacts the city's social life. Interestingly, the gay and lesbian student groups at these schools are highly visible, involved, and proud; they spearhead an impressive range of social, health, and community activities.

Manchester also contains one of Europe's few "gay ghettos," the Gay Village. This area, about three square city blocks, includes most (but not all) of the city's gay bars, shops, and other venues—not the least of which is the fabulous Café Manto (so wonderfully hip that it attracts a straight crowd, too!). Plan to hang around this place. Not only is their coffee mind-blowing, but it's a marvelously reassuring vision of the future—a place where homos, hetties, and everything in between eat, drink, and mix in harmony. Now, for a place with a reputation as gritty as Manchester's ain't that good salve?

One of the nice things about the UK is that it's small enough that you can travel to and fro on a moment's notice.

Rail service between London and Manchester is extremely frequent—every hour, most of the time. And at just under three hours, it's a short enough jaunt to make one night in Manchester (ahem) an easy reality.

HOTELS

HOLIDAY INN CROWNE PLAZA (Peter St.; 236 3333) The best hotel in town. Unlike prefab American Holiday Inns, this one occupies a former old "steamship" hotel. *Eleganza.* EXPENSIVE.

VICTORIA AND ALBERT (Water Street; 832 1188) Not the most central, but the best business hotel, with modern facilities, helpful staff. EXPENSIVE.

BRITTANIA HOTEL (Portland Street; 228 2288) Well-known luxury "warehouse," a large, stylish hotel right in the middle of town. MODERATE.

CHARTERHOUSE (Oxford Street; 236 9999) Imposing old hotel, very atmospheric, and central, too. Nice! MODERATE.

DOMINION HOTEL (Princess Street; 953 1280) Elegant Olde England dinosaur within a stone's throw from the Gay Village—thus, recommended. Fine gym, too. MODERATE.

PORTLAND THISTLE (3–5 Portland Street; 228 3400) One of Manchester's top hotels, if slightly bland. Central location. MODERATE.

HOTEL PICCADILLY (Piccadilly Square; 236 8414) Modern, central hotel with the best pool in town. INEXPENSIVE TO MODERATE.

CASTLEFIELD HOTEL (Liverpool Road; 832 7073) Former YMCA turned hotel on historic site. Best plus: the biggest gym in town, all for a song. INEXPENSIVE.

SACHA's (Tib Street) Incredibly hideous decor in this old tourist hotel, but a cheap, central place to stay. INEXPENSIVE.

CARLTON HOUSE (153 Upper Chorlton Road; 881 4635) Gay hotel cum sauna. OK, but not super-central. INEXPENSIVE.

REMBRANDT HOTEL (Sackville Street; 236 1311) Sleazy, cheap gay hotel. If you must. INEXPENSIVE.

RESTAURANTS

BARNABY RUDGE (Old Bank Street)
Not trendy, but a fun place for an old-style English meal.

BOODLE'S (34 Canal Street)
Art deco. Nouvelle English, often rated the best in town.

BRASSERIE ST. PIERRE (57 Princess Street)
Manchester's crème de la crème; the best French place in town.

CAFÉ BONJOUR (47 Peter Street)
Lovely, informal country French place, cheap and good. Especially recommended for lunchtime.

COCO'S (18 Fountain Street)
Excellent, upmarket Italian place that's a perennial favorite.

COCOTOO (57 Whitworth Street)
Very busy, very "in" Italian place with excellent food and gaw-jus staff. (What more do you need?)

COPACABANA (7 Dale Street)
Brazilian restaurant, often with live music. And cute waiters . . .

DUKE'S 92 (18 Castle Street)
Wine bar in historic old Manchester area. Light lunchtime fare. Cute.

ELVIS'S PALACE (116 London Road, Stockport)
A hoot! Chinese restaurant with Elvis impersonators. Out of town, but worth the trip with a group of friends.

HARRY RAMSDEN'S (1 Water Street)
They say it's the best fish and chips in the world. Who am I to argue?

J.W. JOHNSON'S (78 Deansgate)
Tex-Mex for days. Hip youngish crowd.

LA TASCA (76–78 Deansgate)
Fabulous, delicious Spanish *tapas* place that's attracting a hip, young crowd. Lovely!

PIZZA EXPRESS (6 So. King Street)
Part of a national chain, but for some reason Manchester's branch attracts a hip, young crowd. Good 'za, too!

SIAM ORCHID (54 Portland Street)
Fabulous Thai place. Popular among local foodies.

THE MARKET (104 High Street)
The place to see and be seen. Wonderful Nouvelle English fare. Recommended for that splurge.

THE MONGOLIAN (in Charterhouse Hotel)
Classic do-it-yourself Mongolian BBQ, interesting crowd. (LA readers will know what I mean.)

YANG SING (34 Princess Street)
Not trendy at all, just the best Chinese food in Northern England. If the urge strikes . . .

CAFÉS

ATLAS (376 Deansgate)
Space-age meets early sixties design. One of the coolest places in town; heavy gay involvement.

CORNER HOUSE (70 Oxford Street)
Café-bar on premises of unique cinema complex. Natural foods. Definitely worth a stop.

DRY BAR (28–30 Oldham Street)
Owned by seminal post-punk band New Order; isn't that grooviness enough? Fabulous design.

GREEN ROOM (54–6 Whitworth Street)
Postmodern decor with arty crowd; light lunch fare. Very groovy.

ISOBAR (Afflecks Palace, Oldham Street)
Very cool design—postmodern meets fifties. Especially groovy at night; performances, sometimes.

MANTO'S (46 Canal Street)
Ultra-trendy gay bar/café *cum* hangout for groovy straights. Popular day and (especially) night. Not to be passed by!

NIGHT & DAY (26 Oldham Street)
Homemade English food. Performances, readings on selected days. Cute.

TEN CAFÉ BAR (10 Tariff Street)
> Artsy crowd, nice light lunches. Very Manchester.

SHOPPING

Manchester's shopping scene isn't huge; it's easily covered in its entirety in an afternoon. Here's what you'll find:

KING STREET, ST. ANN'S STREET, and ST. ANN'S SQUARE are for the city's most upscale shops, designer names, and a couple of avant-garde boutiques.

AFFLECK'S PALACE is the grooviest show in town. It was started in 1981 as squatter's stalls, and the city government reluctantly let it evolve into today's format: a multi-story amalgam of young designers' shops, used clothing stores, haircutters, a café, and more. Super-groovy, definitely worth a look.

ROYAL EXCHANGE: Upmarket urban mall; the usual suspects abound.

ARNDALE CENTER: 260 stores in an enclosed center right in the middle of town; shops slant low- to mid-market.

GAY

BARS

AUSTIN's (63 Richmond Street)
Gay/lesbian/trannies; bar/cabaret. Fairly down-market.

BLOOM STREET CAFÉ (39 Bloom)
Gay-run café in the heart of boysville. Worth a visit.

CENTRAL PARK (Sackville Street)
Gay and lesbian bar, fairly popular if untrendy. "Strangeways" party on Saturday is best-attended night.

CRUZ (101 Princess Street)
Manchester's biggest, busiest gay joint. Best weekends, but try during the week.

EQUINOX (Bloom Street)
In the heart of the Gay Village. Theme nights; some better than others. A crap shoot, but a stone's thrown from anywhere else.

NAPOLEON'S (Sackville and Bloom Streets)
Clone crowd's favorite pub.

PADDY'S GOOSE (29 Bloom Street)
Mixed gay/straight pub, less hysterical than most of its neighbors.

Q-BAR (Richmond Street)
Small, busy Euro-style bar; somewhat more sophisticated than the surrounding pubs.

DANCE CLUBS

FLESH (at the Hacienda)
Last Wednesday of every month. Legendary gay party, draws crowds as far as London. Manchester's sine qua non of groovy gaydom.

NEW YORK, NEW YORK (98 Bloom Street)
Upstairs: disco (after 11 P.M.). Downstairs: busy, somewhat sleazy pub. Worth a stop-by.

PARADISE FACTORY (112–116 Princess Street)
The best ongoing gay dance club; a must-do. Open till 4 A.M., weekends.

SLUT HUT (at Home Club)
Gay/lesbian fetish (leather, rubber) night that's way cool (if somewhat odd). Third Wednesdays at Home.

FRANCE

Nice

Nice is more—and less!—glamorous than you think.

It's easy to confuse it with Cannes, its close neighbor—a town that's glitz central for two weeks, then becomes even more tacky (depressed even) after the film crowd goes home. Or to think of it as Monaco, an anachronistic city-state where royals drive off cliffs.

Instead, what Nice is, above all else, is a major metropolitan center—the sixth-largest city in France. Though tourism remains its largest industry, it is more than an overgrown beach town; rather, you're looking at an economic and social center of the Riviera. What Malaga is to Spain, Nice is to France.

Now, don't expect Rome or New York; we're not talking crazed, hectic pace. Nice vehemently retains its Mediterranean style and stance. Plus, a large portion of its year-round residents are retirees—both from France and beyond—so things on all counts move just a bit slow.

But you'll come to Nice for the same reason senior citizens, beach bunnies, and the greatest artists of this century have: the light, the sea, the air. Yes, Nice is commercial; yes, it's too expensive; but it's also one of the great natural settings on earth.

If you arrive after dark, head straight to the main beachfront drag, the Promenade des Anglais. Touristy, yes; overbuilt, sure; still, this is one of the grandest strolls in the world. Look west toward the landmark Hotel Negresco—always a vision in white—and it'll take your breath away. The bottom line: You're going to feel you're somewhere really important and fab. (It's a fine daytime walk, too, but after dark is when you should really first see this street.)

The city's main square, the place Masséna, from which the Promenade emanates, is another sight that'll make you swoon. To the east are shooting fountains of majestic proportions; to the right, an arched sculpture that speaks (to me, at least) of the endlessness of the sky and the sea. If all this sounds disingenuously breathless, please trust me—and once you're there, you'll agree.

What else to do? Old Nice, as you'd expect, is a lazy labyrinth of winding streets, and features shops (cool and touristy), restaurants, and (fairly laborious) drinking spots. Twilight is the most atmospheric time to take the tour, as it infinitely heightens the sensation of long ago and far away. Then, take a cruise on the cours Saléya and choose a seafood restaurant, either one of mine recommended below or the gem you find on your own.

Though Nice is above all a place to enjoy the sensual pleasures, take an afternoon off from your cretinous path and tour its two world-class picture palaces. The Post-Impressionists, especially, made Nice their base, and used the interplay of sky and sea (oh God, I'm sounding like one of those hideous suburban women at the Museum of Modern Art) to glorious—and dizzyingly different—effect. ("It represents man's inhumanity to man, dahling!'')

Speaking of men, Nice's are reason enough to spend a few days here. About half the population is of Italian ancestry, another quarter is mixed Franco-Italian, and the results are stunning. But caveat emptor: As in any monied resort, hustlers abound, so be careful (if not frugal). Your money, your choice (as Peter Jennings likes to say!). In any case, Nice is a tacky, terrific, totally Mediterranean paradise everyone must visit once.

HOTELS

NEGRESCO (37, promenade des Anglais; 93 88 00 58) One of the most architecturally magnificent hotels in the world and a focal point of Nice society—a great, white whale on the beach. Must be seen to be believed. VERY EXPENSIVE.

BEAU-RIVAGE (24, rue St. François de Paule; 93 80 80 70) Gorgeous Belle Epoque palace, part of the famous chain. A luxury indeed. VERY EXPENSIVE.

GRAND HOTEL ASTOR (12, avenue Félix-Faure; 93 80 62 52) Off the Espace Masséna, Nice's most majestic square. A big, hulking, fabulous cruise ship of a hotel. EXPENSIVE.

WEST END NICE (31, promenade des Anglais; 93 88 79 91) Turn-of-the-century facade, modernized rooms

on the main beachside drag. Recommended. EXPEN-
SIVE.

BRICE (44, rue Maréchal-Joffre 93 88 14 44) Lovely
old charmer in "downtown" Nice—a great, unexor-
bitant choice. MODERATE.

HOTEL LE GRIMALDI (15, rue Grimaldi; 93 87 73 61)
Nice, basic, moderately priced hotel in the middle of
"New" Nice. MODERATE.

LE PETIT PALAIS (10, avenue Emile Bieckert 93 62
19 11) Not central, but a charming hillside location
atop the old part of town. Worth considering for the
views. MODERATE.

ATHENA (11, rue Paul Déroulède; 93 88 03 19) Decent two-star hotel with central location its real drawing
card. INEXPENSIVE.

DE BERNE (1, avenue Thiers; 93 88 25 08) Small, no-
frills hostelry for budgeteers. INEXPENSIVE.

NEW YORK (44, avenue Maréchal-Foch; 93 92 04 19)
Charming exterior, redone rooms; central location for
a song. INEXPENSIVE.

RESTAURANTS

AU MOULIN ENCHANTÉ (1, rue Barberis)
    Delightful eatery with Niçois specialties galore.

BRASSERIE FLO (4, rue Sacha Guitry)
Somewhat staid, but worth seeing for former theatrical decor. Part of Flo French chain.

CAVE NIÇOISE (5, rue Masséna)
Traditional decor and food. Slightly, but not oppressively, touristy.

CHOU-CHOUX (6, avenue Maraldi)
Cute little restaurant with a gay clientele. Atmosphere outdoes food.

DAVIA (11 bis, rue Grimaldi)
Cheap, but awfully good, unpretentious little place. 60F menu's a steal!

LA PETITE MAISON (11, rue St. François de Paule)
Traditional Niçois specialties in a much-loved local setting. A nice institution.

L'AVION BLEU (10, rue Alphonse Karr)
Modern decor and food. Upscale chic.

LE BARON IVRE (6, rue Maraldi)
Lovely, gay-friendly restaurant with wonderful local fare. Give it a try!

LE COEUR DE VENISE (22, rue Benoît-Bonico)
Exotic decor, with specialties from around the world. A real original.

LE COMPTOIR (20, rue St. François de Paule)
Elegant eatery famed for its Niçois fare. Highly recommended.

LE FROG (3, rue Milton Robbins)
French interpretation of American foods: ribs, burgers, etc. Very "in."

LE GRAND CAFE DES ARTS (Place Yves Klein)
Trendy, modern lunch spot in the Modern Art Museum. Worth a look-see.

LE SAFARI (cours Saléya)
Young, semi-trendy, and *très décontracté*. Niçois cooking (again).

LES DENTS DE LA MER (2, rue cours Saléya)
Expensive, trendy fish restaurant with nonpareil *fruits de mer*. Very good!

TAVERNE DU CHATEAU (42, rue Droite)
Cozy, cheap restaurant in the heart of Old Town. Local color galore.

TEXAS COYOTE (Place Garibaldi)
Tex-Mex café for hip Nice boys and girls.

SHOPPING

What with its high concentration of internationalists and moneyed retirees, Nice offers a bounty of high-priced shopping fare. Most of this activity is centered in the *centre-ville*, specifically the rues Paradis, Alphonse Karr, and Verdun. Women's shops are prevalent—along with the expected rash of overpriced hair joints—but a smattering of men's stuff can be found as well.

The avenue Jean-Médecin is where you'll find the less economically favored shops—there's a Galeries Lafayette, C & A, and (to the Niçois, inexplicably, a source of huge civic pride) a Marks and Spencer, whose ill-fitting British sweaters now seem to be invading the world.

A fabulous branch of agnès b. can be found in old Nice at 17, rue des Ponchettes. The streets of this quarter also house a jagged collection of postpunk Spandex, African, and just plain touristy shops—but it's fun to browse here anyway.

In sum, there's not much to rival Paris's best shops, but die-hard spendthrifts will find enough to amuse them if shop they must!

GAY

First, a warning: the gay scene in Nice is awfully *cher*. A beer in one of the drinking bars listed below will set you back five bucks; entry to a disco is $12 (during the week) to $20 (by week's end). So bring a lot of cash, or don't go out at all! (On the plus side, you don't see guys thrashing around bars smashed out of their minds—economics sees to that.)

BARS

L'ASCENSEUR (18, rue Emmanuel Philibert)
Pleasant video bar with a couple of rooms with banquettes; Sunday is karaoke night (if you can carry a tune, you win).

LE RUSCA (2, rue Rusca)
Small drinkery in the port area. Open from 5:00 P.M. on.

LE TRAP (avenue Risson, across from Bowling-Acropolis)
Small video bar with amicable clientele, best late.

DANCE CLUBS

BLUE BOY (9, rue Spinetta)
Nice's most popular disco. Two bars, video, strobes. Disco heaven!

FACTORY (8, quai Lunel)
Techno palace with mixder, though mostly gay, very trendy crowd.

LE QUARTZ (18, rue des Congrès)
Most centrally located disco; best on Friday and Saturday nights. Entry is pricey indeed!

SAUNAS

LE GRAND BLEU (7, avenue Désambrois)
LE SEPT (7, rue Foncet)

Paris

Several inalienable truths:

1. Paris is the most beautiful city in the world.
2. French cuisine is fabulous.
3. French men are (often) incredibly sexy and (usually) have no concept of fidelity whatsoever.
4. Parisians *are* rude to people who don't speak French. But since everyone *should,* they have a point.
5. Visit Paris and you'll never want to leave.

Think the above is oversimplified, contradictory, or just plain dumb? You're probably right on all counts. Writing about Paris is like describing sex or love or taxicabs. If, as an adult, you don't know why all these things are great, I can hardly tell you now.

So let's get one thing straight (as it were): I am a stupid, intransigent, dyed-in-the-wool Francophile, and have no time for anyone who is not. (Sorry—this is one personal prejudice that I can't get over.) The first book I ever bought as a tyke—who knows why?—was something called *Learn to Say It in French.* I majored in French, went to the Sorbonne, and buy *Paris Match* magazine even when I don't have anything to eat. (The

West Hollywood library, my former reading room, has *Match* jetted in weekly; no such luck at my East Village barrio branch.)

All this is to say that whatever I say here can never be near an objective point of view. But why should it be; and what could I possibly say about Paris that hasn't been said before? You've got your Seine, you've got your fashion and food, you've got your kul-tcha, plus sex galore. I mean, what the fuck else is there?

So rather than wax poetic about any of the above—you'll be able to do that once you arrive—I'm doing something else instead. To wit: giving you a list of sundry and varied recommendations on enjoying Paris that, I hope, only a former resident could give you. Here goes:

A. If you've never been before, sign up for a three- or four-hour city tour. (No, the bus will not be full of Germans and Japanese—they sit in their own buses, and speak their own language.)

B. Yes, it is a touristy thing to do, but it's still the best way to get your grounding in a totally new place. (Some guidebooks tell you that Paris is, geographically, small. Don't believe it for a minute. The city covers a lot of ground, and you'll want to see it all.)

C. Write down your top ten attraction must-dos (Louvre, Les Invalides, Les Tuileries, Les Champs-Elysées, La Comédie Française, etc.)

Then, distribute them among the number of days you're going to be in town. But . . . be sure to leave either the morning or afternoon (preferably the latter) of each day free to do any of the following: walk aimlessly about (the most fun thing you can do in Paris, methinks); sleep off a huge lunch; go to a sauna (much less sleazy in France than in the States, since they inevitably have a vaguely therapeutic or gymnastic air); or tank up on caffeine in an inviting café. Note: Do not under any circumstances order decaf or ask for nonfat milk—better yet, don't ask for milk at all, except in the morning—or complain about people smoking *en plein air*. Take it like a man or stay at home. Remember, the French are Latins and would rather "go like Elsie" (sorry, Liza) than live to be a hundred and have Willard Scott talk about how they're gorgeous and love to garden.

D. Go to the movies. If, at first blush, this sounds asinine, just hear me out. Cinema is the French national pastime, and Paris's range of theaters—more per capita than anywhere else in the world—is legendary. No, you don't have to see a Jerry Lewis film (his importance to modern-day France is exaggerated, anyway). Go to the movies for these reasons: (1) it's a really French thing to do; (2) you'll doubtlessly find, in *Pariscope* (the weekly guide to Parisian events), some old flick not available on video that you thought would never surface again (in my case, Joan Crawford in *Queen Bee*—a nonstop hoot!); (3) French cinemas (mostly) now have popcorn and (sometimes) *real butter;* and (4) movie theaters, especially small ones, are the best places to meet boys (at least the black-garbed, Gauloise-puffing Genet devotees I favor).

E. Hang out in the Marais. More than just Paris's gay center, it's a focal point of gay life for all of Europe. One of the oldest sections of Paris, the Marais was, for many years, home to the Jewish ghetto. With the erection (sorry!) of the Centre Pompidou (also known as Beaubourg) at the site of the former Les Halles market, the entire area became the home of Paris's bohemian and avant-garde life.

Up until the early 80s, Paris's gay scene was lively, but very much underground—out-of-the-way locations, expensive entry fees, and doors bedecked with the warning "Club Prive." Happily, changes in societal mores (both French and international) have permitted the explosion of gay culture throughout *la capitale*. Nowhere is this more in evidence than in the Marais, whose cafes, shops, bars, and restaurants flourish. From a midday meal to afternoon coffee to night-time revelry, the Marais beckons with a heady mix—the best of French gay life.

That, dear readers, is my advice. It's at once heart-felt and superfluous, since no one can visit Paris and not have an incredible time. *Amusez-vous bien!*

With their flagship the *TGV (Train à Grande Vitesse)*, French trains are a pleasure and a joy—clean, punctual, a great way to see *les provinces.* To get to Nice, Toulouse, or almost anywhere in Western Europe, you may want to consider a Flexipass, which allows fifteen individual days of travel within a two-month period of use. Available in first and second class, the Flexipass is a winning way to travel; and, though reservations on some trains are de rigueur, it certainly makes getting around a breeze. (Thanks to Minitel, France's state-of-the-art national computer program, almost any concierge has a schedule of trains at his or her fingertips, and can tell you which ones require reservations in advance.)

Rail Europe, the consortium that represents the national railroads of countries throughout the Continent, has offices in New York, Boston, Boulder, Chicago, Dallas, Miami, Minneapolis, Montreal, Philadelphia, Santa Monica, San Francisco, Seattle, Toronto, Vancouver, and White Plains, NY. Call for the information and prices you need.

HOTELS

LANCASTER (7, rue de Berri, 8ème; 40 76 40 76 or, in the U.S., (800) 447-7462) Legendary home of Dietrich, Tina Turner, kings and queens. Former *hôtel de ville* turned hyper-exclusive, very correct address. The pinnacle of luxury! (Beg, steal, or borrow . . .) VERY EX-PENSIVE.

CRILLON (10, place de la Concorde, 8ème; 42 65 24 24) One of Paris's palace hotels, where luxury and quiet elegance are one. Très chic, and then some. VERY EXPENSIVE.

MEURICE (228, rue de Rivoli, 1er; 42 60 38 60) Slightly less expensive than the big names, yet with all their correctness and style. Fabulous location and mar-velous staff. VERY EXPENSIVE.

RITZ (15, place Vendôme, 1ème; 42 60 38 30) What can I say? One of the world's grandest and most fash-ionable hotels. Do whatever it takes! VERY EXPENSIVE.

MONTALEMBERT (3, avenue Montalembert, 7ème; 45 58 68 11) A fave among fashion and artsy types, a splendid small hotel in the best part of the 7th. EXPEN-SIVE.

BALZAC (6, rue Balzac, 8ème; 45 61 97 22) Super-charming, private hotel with perfect off-the-Champs-Elysées location. (Also, home of chic Bice restaurant.) EXPENSIVE.

LUTETIA (45, boulevard Raspail, 6ème; 45 44 38 10) Belle Epoque masterpiece between Montparnasse and St.-Germain des Prés, perfect for lovers of the Left Bank. EXPENSIVE.

HOTEL DE LA BRETONNERIE (22, rue Ste.-Croix-de-la-Bretonnerie, 4ème; 48 87 77 63) Perhaps the Marais's best choice: a charming three-star gem, rather more respectable than its neighbors. MODERATE.

NOVOTEL (8, place Marguerite de Navarre, 1er; 42 21 31 31) Part of the generic French chain, rather like a minimalist Holiday Inn. Charmless efficiency, yet its Les Halles location makes up for a multitude of sins. MODERATE.

ANGLETERRE (44, rue Jacob, 6ème; 45 44 38 11) Small gem in the former British embassy—and so close to Le Trap (see page 96)! MODERATE.

JEU DE PAUME (54, rue St.-Louis-en-Ile, 4ème; 43 26 14 18) Really cool hotel on the Ile St.-Louis, blending old and new design. Nice! MODERATE.

ST.-MERRY (78, rue de la Verronerie, 4ème; 42 78 14 15) Faux-medieval decor is a hoot, if only for Anne Rice fans. And so close to the bars! MODERATE.

HOTEL CENTRAL DU MARAIS (33, rue Vieille du Temple, 4ème; 48 87 56 08) Paris's only real gay hotel, just above the eponymous bar. Very basic, with marginal amenities and facilities (rather like a rooming house, in fact). INEXPENSIVE.

HOTEL DE LA PLACE DES VOSGES (12, rue de Birague, 4ème; 42 72 60 46) Nice, if basic, little place in the least frenetic part of the Marais. Recommended. INEXPENSIVE.

HOTEL DES BATIGNOLLES (26–8, rue des Batignolles, 17ème; 43 87 70 40) Very simple one-star hotel in the emergingly chic 17th. A bargain, and not without some charm. INEXPENSIVE.

ESMERELDA (4, rue St.-Julien-le-Pauvre, 5ème; 43 54 19 20) Distinctly Gothic air—why not, since it's so close to Notre-Dame? A cheap old standby, still good. INEXPENSIVE.

LE VIEUX MARAIS (8, rue du Platre, 4ème; 42 78 47 22) Nice if unfancy Marais hotel. INEXPENSIVE.

RESTAURANTS

AU QUAI D'ORSAY (49, quai d'Orsay, 7ème)
Wonderful, traditional bourgeois cooking in fashionable setting. Delicieux!

BICE (6, rue Balzac, 8ème)
Paris branch of chic international Italian "chain."

LA COUPOLE (102, boulevard de Montparnasse, 14ème)
I know, I know—how obvious. Still, everyone should eat here once . . .

LA MAISON (1, rue de Bûcherie, 5ème)
Perhaps Paris's most "in" restaurant right now: entertainment and fashion types abound. For trendseekers, a must.

LA ROTISSERIE DU BEAUJOLAIS (19, quai de la Tournelle, 5ème)
From the owner of the famed La Tour d'Argent, a cheaper (not much), trendier version with first-rate food.

LA TELEGRAPHE (41, rue de Lille, 7ème)
Trendy crowd, night after night. Kinda "model food," though. Chic, chic, chic.

LE BISTROT A COTE FLAUBERT (10, rue Gustave Flaubert, 17ème)
Two Michelin stars for this archetypically haute cuisine place.

LE PETIT GAVROCHE (42, rue Ste.-Croix-de-la-Bretonnerie, 4ème)
Very popular, inexpensive, unpretentious Marais eatery with a mostly gay crowd.

LE PETIT PICARD (42, rue Ste.-Croix-de-la-Bretonnerie, 4ème)
Wonderful, friendly place. French fare in the heart of "Guyville."

ORANGERIE (28, rue St.-Louis-en-Ile, 4ème)
Jovial joint with good food (dinner only) and cinematic/theatrical crowd.

PAUL (15, place Dauphine, 1er)
Good, cheap, tasty bistro fare.

TABLE D'ANVERS (2, place d'Anvers, 9ème)
Out-of-the-way but worth the trip. The newest gastronomic marvel in Paris. Say you've been!

YVAN (1 bis, rue Jean-Mermoz, 8ème)
Very *branché,* very "now." A place of the moment, indeed.

GAY-FRIENDLY RESTAURANTS

Anyone can eat anywhere in Paris, but the following restaurants actively seek a gay clientele. Go and hold your boyfriend's hand . . .

GAI MOULIN (4, rue St.-Merri, 4ème)
Gay-intensive eatery featuring excellent French provincial fare. Lovely!

L'AMAZONIAL (3, rue Ste.-Opportuité, 1er)
Brazilian-influenced cuisine; lively, hooty place.

L'AVIATIC (23, rue Ste.-Croix-de-la-Bretonnerie, 4ème)
Mixed but gay-friendly crowd, Continental fare.

L'EGLANTINE (9, rue de la Verrerie, 4ème.)
Busy bistro, in the middle of the Marais. You must . . .

LE PETIT PRINCE (12, rue de Lanneau, 5ème)
Fab French food and practically all-boy clientele in the heart of the 5th. Go!

NANTUCKET CAFÉ (37, rue du Roi de Sicile, 4ème)
Trendy "resto" best for lightish fare and pretty boys.

XICA DA SILVA (47, rue des Batignolles, 17ème)
High-spirited Brazilian place with large gay following. *Muito bom!*

Special Note: Of course, the most fun of all is wandering around Paris and finding that special place you fall in love with and tell all your friends about. So use the above as a guide, but don't let it set your dining plans in stone. Trust your own instincts, and chances are that the special place you just happen upon will be a gem. After all, the adage "It's hard to get a bad meal in Paris" really is true!

CAFÉS

CAFÉ BEAUBOURG (rue St.-Martin, across from the Centre Beaubourgler)
> Vies with the Costes for the title of chichi café #1. A very cool place to meet friends, or to hang out with the *Herald Tribune* on a sunny afternoon.

CAFÉ COSTES (4, rue Berger, 1er)
> *The* café for the artsy/boho/fashion crowd. Expensive, but an afternoon's delight.

LE DOME (108, boulevard du Montparnasse, 14ème)
> Perhaps the least pretentious sitting-spot on the boulevard de Montparnasse; the ghost of Hemingway still haunts.

LE FLORE (172, boulevard St.-Germain, 5ème)
> Before there was the Marais, Le Flore was an unofficial daytime gathering spot for artsy and fashion fags. It still retains its erstwhile pissy air, but it's as big a landmark as they come.

LE SELECT (99, boulevard de Montparnasse, 14ème)
> Another classic Montparnasse spot—past its heyday, but a legend still.

LES DEUX MAGOTS (170 boulevard St.-Germain, 5ème)
> Pricey, and perhaps no longer the intelligentsia's

watering hole, but a traditional favorite in St.-Germain des Prés nontheless.

AU FEU (12, rue St.-Simon, 4ème)
Fun new snackery in the Marais. Try it!

COFFEE SHOP (3, rue Ste.-Croix-de-la-Bretonnerie, 1er)
A must: the Marais's flagship gay café. Cute food and boys, all day long.

HOTEL CENTRAL (33, rue Vielle du Temple, 4ème)
A landmark, the place that single-handedly started the Marais as the gay mecca of France. Perfect for a beer or coffee in the late afternoon.

SHOPPING

Paris is the world capital of shopping; in no other city do you see as many people schlepping around with glossy bags. And why not? Looking good is the national obsession of the French; they remain the best put-together people in the world.

The coolest place to *faire des cours* is in the Marais, specifically in the shops centered around the Place des Vosges. (The rue des Francs Bourgeois and St. Antoine are the key names here.) The shopping scene also creeps into the gay part of the Marais, though the stretched-tight fagwear may be too chichi for some.

Don't fail to visit the underground mall at the

Centre Beaubourg in Les Halles, which can occupy the better part of an afternoon. Funky, young-slanting fashions abound, and sexy mall rats make for cute cruising indeed.

For big-name designers at top-dollar (franc?) prices, the rue due Faubourg-St.-Honoré and the avenue Montaigne are king (queen?). Department store fans will want to visit Au Printemps and Galeries Lafayette, which have not only menswear but everything else under the sun (various locations around town).

Like a bargain? Then head for the rue d'Alésia in the 14th, where designers and moderately priced haberdashers have outlet stores; though know in advance that they're usually last season's goods.

GAY

No doubt about it, Paris is the gay capital of Europe right now. The reasons why should prove no mystery at all. Paris has always been a magnificent city nonpareil (you read the intro to this chapter, I hope!); and, when city government liberalized sufficiently to permit the establishment of endless gay clubs, meeting houses, saunas, and more, gays from all over the world flocked to the burgeoning scene. Amsterdam's prominence in the seventies as a gay mecca stemmed more from the possibilities for open gay life than anything inherent in the city itself—I mean, it's utterly lovely, but not quite the fashion and financial city Paris has always been. If Paris has any rival to the throne, it would have to be Barcelona, very happening right now; but the range and variety of gay life in Paree is, in my book, second to none. The mere scope of this list is testament to that:

BARS

AMNESIA (42, rue Vieille du Temple, 4ème)
Hyper-trendy bar/café with tasty daily specials. New and cute.

BANANA CAFÉ (13, rue de la Ferronnerie, 1er)
Mixed, semi-trendy joint, open very late. Better to visit with a pal than alone.

CAFÉ MOUSTACHE (138, rue St.-Martin, 10ème)
Older, mustachioed crowd, somewhat working class.

LA LUNA (28, rue Keller, 11ème)
Sexy, ultra-cruisy bar near the Bastille, best after midnight. Really hot!

LE BAR (5, rue de la Ferronnerie, 1er)
Steamy, multilevel, very cruisy new bar. Busy from around 9:30 P.M. on. Smooching in the shadows . . .

LE BAR DU PALMIER (16, rue des Lombards, 1er)
Mixed (read: uncruisy) new cocktail bar. You be the judge.

LE BAR DE LA PLAGE (12, rue Colonel Oudot, 12ème)
>Trendy, mixed bar, open after-hours (i.e., later than 5 A.M.) on weekends. A scene!

LE KELLER (14, rue Keller, 11ème)
>Paris's busiest and best-known leather bar.

LE MAJESTIC (34, rue Vieille du Temple, 4ème)
>Mixed, but heavily gay-attended bar/restaurant. Young, sexy trendoids galore. Fun!

LE MANHATTAN (8, rue des Anglais, 5ème)
>Seventies holdout, a shadow of its former sexy self. Dancing (and more crowded) on weekends.

LE MARGINAL (2, rue Lamandé, 17ème)
>Trendy new mixed bar in the newly chic 17th. Try it with straight friends.

LE PIANO ZINC (19, rue des Blancs Manteaux, 4ème)
>Piano bar, *au français.* Boys and girls, usually older.

LES PLANCHES (36, rue Doudeauville, 18ème)
>Kitschy new club with a seaside feel. Mixed, but lots of boys.

LE QUETZAL (10, rue de la Verrerie, 4ème)
>The ne plus ultra of the Marais. Very busy after work; a great place to start an evening of clubby rounds.

LE SUBWAY (35, rue Ste-Croix-de-la-Bretonnerie, 4ème)

> Busy new Marais drinking spot, best in the early evenings. Slightly sleazy crowd mixed with just plain guys.

LE TRANSFERT (3, rue de la Sourdière, 1er)

> Leather and lace.

LE TRAP (10, rue Jacob, 6ème)

> Paris's steamiest bar, with very naughty goings-on upstairs. *Vive la France!*

LE WAF (35, rue Davy, 17ème)

> Out-of-the-way, working-class fagbar; only if you're staying in the 17th.

MEC ZONE (27, rue Turgot, 9ème)

> Warm leatherettes.

MIC MAN (24, rue Geoffroy l'Angevin, 4ème)

> Older, chummy Marais crowd. Touchy-feely downstairs room.

DANCE CLUBS

B.H. (7, rue de la Roule, 1er)

> One of Paris's longest-running gay clubs, a cavernous smokehouse with a sexy feel. Best late.

FOLIES PIGALLE (Place Pigalle 18ème)
Trendy, mixed night scene with groovy, hip boys galore.

LE CLUB (14, rue St.-Denis 1er)
Twinkietown.

L'INSOLITE (33, rue des Petits Champs, 1er)
OK dance hall.

LE PALACE (8, rue Faubourg Montmartre, 9ème)
Sunday tea dance attracts Paris's foxiest lads. Hot, hot, hot!

LE QUEEN (102, avenue des Champs-Elysees, 8ème)
How's this for progress—a gay club right on the Champs-Elysées! London-style technoteria for the hip young crowd.

LES BAINS (7, rue Bourg l'Abbe, 3ème)
Mixed dance club for international trendies. Check for all-gay nights.

LE SCARAMOUCHE (44, rue Vivienne, 2ème)
All-night gay dancing, best toward weekends.

LE SCORPION (25, boulevard Poissonnière, 2ème)
Hot dance joint, very sexy crowd.

REXCLUB (5, boulevard Poissonnière, 2ème)
Trendy, mixed-gender dance club.

THE NEW LOOK (40, rue des Blancs Manteaux, 4ème)

    Just-opened danceteria; too soon to tell, but looks to be hot and hip.

SAUNAS

EUROMEN'S CLUB (8, rue St.-Marc, 2ème)
IDM (4, rue du Faubourg-Montmartre, 2ème)
KEY WEST (141, rue Lafayette, 10ème)
KING (21, rue Bridaine, 17ème)
LE MANDALA (2, rue Drouot, 9ème)
LE MYKONOS (71, rue des Martyrs, 18ème)
LE TILT (41, rue Ste.-Anne, 1er)
UNIVERS GYM (20, rue des Bons Enfants, 1er)

Toulouse

Everything that's best about France is found in one massive dose in Toulouse. Close your eyes and imagine the perfect provincial city—say, from one of Rohmer's early films—and you're probably thinking of Toulouse.

Locals call their city the Florence of France, and in many ways the comparison couldn't be more correct. About equal in population, sophistication (very!), and age, the two cities have practically everything Rome and Paris have—plus more joie de vivre and far less attitude. Need proof that the French can be supernice? Spend one afternoon in Toulouse and you'll be convinced.

(Here, a footnote: Surprisingly, Toulouse's sister city isn't Florence, but—get this!—Atlanta; however, no one could tell me why. Georgian readers: tell all, do.)

Fourth among French cities in population, after Paris, Marseille, and Lyon, Toulouse beats all but the first in warmth and charm. Marseille is dingy and Lyon oppressively bourgeois, so take it from a hardened Francophile, and ditch 'em both for the best-kept touristic secret in La Belle France. (By all means, Toulouse is worth a trip in itself, but it's also the perfect rest stop on the road to Spain.) The city's loci of interest can easily be covered in a couple of days—though, if time is no object, you may easily be seduced into stretching your visit out a day longer still.

On the subject of sloth, you'll soon find out that Toulousains are proud of the kinder, gentler pace of their lives, especially when compared to the whirlwind of Paree. That said, Toulouse is far from laid-back: It's the aeronautics center of France (the Airbus Industrie factory is worth a tour, even if the mere idea seems too butch for words), and an economic powerhouse to boot—many high-tech concerns are centered here. Plus, it's the second largest student center in France, a fact that adds to the town's lively air.

The final word: Toulouse is a cosmopolitan, up-beat, prosperous city that has beckoned France's best for years. For all these reasons, it should beckon a visit from you as well.

HOTELS

LE GRAND HOTEL DE L'OPERA (1, place du Capitole; 61 21 82 66) Toulouse's best address recalls the days of Madame Bovary. (And you'll love the lobby's "Sensurround" powdered air!) The tiny singles make this hotel moderate; otherwise . . . EXPENSIVE.

LE GRAND HOTEL CAPOUL (13, place Wilson; 61 10 70 70) Really cool! Faux-tropical lobby decor picks up on Toulouse's natural light and turns it into a festive mood. Art exhibitions, often. Favored by fashion crowd. HIGH MODERATE.

ALTEA HOTEL LES CAPITOULS (29, allées Jean-Jaurès; 61 62 63 63) No-nonsense three-star hotel preferred by business types and tourists alike. Modern rooms and facilities. The staff is super-nice. MODERATE.

HOTEL DU GRAND BALCON (8, rue Romiguières; 61 21 48 08) An institution in French history, this is where long-distance flyers—even St.-Exupéry!—decamped before heading off to Africa. Charming old place, with rooms in all price categories, but basically . . . MODERATE.

HOTEL DES BEAUX-ARTS (1, place Pont-Neuf; 61 23 40 50) Where visiting actors and politicos stay. OK modern decor. MODERATE.

HOTEL CASTELLANE (17, rue Castellane; 61 62 18 82) Right off the place Wilson. Pleasant if undistinguished rooms. INEXPENSIVE.

HOTEL ANATOLE FRANCE (46, place Anatole-France) Bare bones, but fine for super-budgeteers. INEXPENSIVE.

RESTAURANTS

AU GASCON (9, rue des Jacobins)
Stick-to-the-ribs Gascogne fare, popularly priced. For the manhandler in you.

BROOKLYN BRIDGE CAFÉ (2, avenue Atlanta)
Toulouse's version of an American joint. Worth a look to hoot—especially at Mickey Rourke motorcycle clones. What a love/hate relationship we have with the frogs!

CHEZ EMILE (13, place St.-Georges)
Specialties of the region that change seasonally; menu prices are always a good value. One of Toulouse's best.

L'ASTARAC (21, rue Perchepinte)
A great date place, in the middle of Old Toulouse—plus, Gascogne cooking at its finest. Very French!

L'ASSIETTE ROSE (10, rue des Blanches)
The menu at 125F is a steal, and the place is lovely. A perennial local favorite.

LE BISTROT DES VINS (5, rue Riguepels)
Specialties are *charcuterie* and *pot-au-feu,* but the wine selection here is really the thing. Cute.

LE COLOMBIER (14, rue Bayard)
Cassoulet comes from Toulouse, and this is as good as it gets. Love dem beans!

LES BEAUX ARTS (1, quai de la Dourade)
Classic Belle Epoque style brasserie, among the most popular places in town. Highly recommended.

LES CAVES DE LA MARECHALE (3, rue Jules-Chalande)

Splendid old room dates from the seventeenth century, and a fabulous value today—especially for 70F menu at lunch. Fish especially good.

LES JARDINS DU GRAND CAFÉ DE L'OPERA (1, place du Capitole)

A must! Lovely garden in Toulouse's chicest hotel, with one of the best chefs in town. Oyster bar is king. Very expensive, but a worthy splurge.

LES JARDINS DE LI (9, rue Croix-Baragon)

The 55F menu is a steal, and this small place in a charming courtyard is a must-do. Why can't you eat like this in the U.S. for ten bucks?

VANEL (22, rue Maurice Fonvielle)

Long-running culinary hit known for its *formule bistrot* at about $20—or, equally, for its pricier menus. A good choice!

CAFÉS

Every square—or, in the case of la place Wilson, oval—has its devotees; only you can find the place for you. Wherever you end up, café-sitting in Toulouse is serious sport; be prepared to make it a focal point of your stay.

The place du Capitole, the city's largest square (and home to an all-day-long flea market) slants young, especially at the student/boho Le Florida (#12)—quite possibly, the smokiest café in the world. (Even LA doesn't have smog this thick—O healthy ones, beware!) The Bibent (#5) is more subdued, and boasts fabulous rococo wall work.

The place St.-Georges, rather more bourgeois, is nonetheless a lovely place to sit, especially at the Van Gogh (#2), with a distinctly Italianate ambience, and Wallace (#15), the more intimate of the two. Alternately, the Café Basque is a great place to watch oldsters play *boules* on the lawn. Or check out the place Wilson's La Frégate (#16), a slightly staid yet sunny *terrasse*.

Two other choices: Café Classico (37, rue des Filatiers) is upscale hip. Café Belge (25, boulevard Strasbourg) has Belgian beer (delish!) and the best *frites* in Toulouse.

SHOPPING

Block by block, the best shopping in France. Here, presentation is everything, and only Florence can match the whimsy, correctness, and charm of Toulouse's shops.

The old city is eminently walkable, and you'll easily find the essentials yourself. As a guide, the most fashionable shops are located between the place Wilson and place Esquirol and their arteries—notably, St. Antoine du T. and the rue de Lafayette. One store trendoids will not want to miss is Zaza (on the place St.-Georges), which has the best of Gaultier, Montana, and their avant-garde ilk.

The galleries of Toulouse are known throughout France, and with good reason—much of the art is first-rate, and often incorporates the local sun and city-scapes. Unlike SoHo snots, gallery personnel here are delighted to have you come in and admire their artists' work, and you may even find yourself schlepping a piece home.

GAY

A new rightist mayor has closed some of Toulouse's erstwhile gay spots, but locals don't seem too scared—"*Ça changera,*" a bartender advised. Anyway, it's just as easy to meet guys in cafés, shops, or on the street—Toulousains are friendly sorts indeed. For clubbing, the following applies:

BARS

DIAGONAL (37, places des Carmes)
Hyper-chic, mixed bar. Trendoids, take note! Way cool.

L'ARTCOR (6, rue de la Colombette)
Trendy, young art bar, best after 11:30 P.M. Eric, the bartender, is a god!

LE BROADWAY (11, rue des Puits-Clos)
Not really a gay venue, but some boys dig the tepid drag revue. Hardly fabulous.

LE QUINQUINA (26, rue Peyras)
Hip, mixed—but heavily gay—bar. Big fun.

Dance Clubs

LE NEW SHANGAI (12, rue de la Pomme)
Only real gay dance club in town. (Even so, there's a gay side and a straight side. See if *you* can tell them apart!)

NYC DISCOTHEQUE (83, allée Charles de Fitte)
Macho, macho men . . . dancing, too. Rumored to close soon, so approach with caution.

Saunas

CALYPSO (16, rue Bayard)
LE PRESIDENT (38, rue Alsace-Lorraine)
PHYSIC CLUB (14, rue d'Aubuisson)

GERMANY

Hamburg

Rainy, gray, and northern, Hamburg looks bleak for days on end, then—*kerpooft!*—the sun turns it into an enchanting harbor town.

Even when the sky is clear, water is everywhere: Hamburg boasts three rivers, countless canals, and—most enticingly—the Alster Lakes. Long called the Venice of the North (a namesake I'd given to Copenhagen or Amsterdam first), Hamburg is also a major port, Germany's gateway to the world (or so the saying goes).

Outside the city center, Hamburg is also incredibly green, with more parks than any other German town, a fact of which the residents are duly proud. My friend from the tourist board proclaimed his love for York, but called it a "concrete jungle"; Hamburg, Europe's best, is wet, lush, and green.

Unlike Munich, Hamburg is anything but a It's a "real" city, with the best and worst of urb The best: glittering shops, lakeside estates, a verse cultural scene. The worst: disgruntle grants, disgruntled Germans (especially the class, who fairly loathe the former group), a dose of addicts and ho's. (Tired-looking pr th runny eyeliner and tacky boots line the l vntown streets; as for *les boys,* there are more pay-for-play bars in Hamburg than anywhere else I've seen. *Sehr* Thomas Mann, no?)

Since it is the communications capital of Germany—the publishing, advertising, and media worlds are all here—Hamburg has its trendy side, too. This is best reflected in the restaurant scene, full of upscale eateries, and in its endless shopping spots. Granted, it's not as "alternative" as Berlin (what is?), but Hamburg definitely has its groovy side.

Hamburg's gay scene is good—not great—but offers enough variety for all but the most hopeless bar hag. Actually, far more interesting than the nightspots are the cafés, especially Gnosa, Mistral, and des Artistes. They're marvy places to while away an afternoon, and they become even more jovial (cruisy, even) at night.

Berlin and Munich may have better publicity machines, but Hamburg has its very own lures. The sophisticated traveler will avoid them at his own cost!

HOTELS

ATLANTIC KEMPINSKI (An der Alster 72–79; 247129) Incredibly grand; you expect to see La Dietrich slither in at any moment. One of the world's great hotels, on the lake near St. Georg. VERY EXPENSIVE.

VIER JAHRESZEITEN (Neuer Jungfernstieg 14–19; 3494602) Another legend, right on Lake Alster. Impossibly correct, even prim. Considered the best hotel in Germany by many. VERY EXPENSIVE.

EUROPAEISCHER HOF (45 Kirchenalle; 248248) Very Old World; excellent location, and far less stuffy than the two above. EXPENSIVE.

RENAISSANCE (Grosse Bleichen; 349180) Castle-like exterior, Art Nouveau interior; the upscale side of the Ramada chain. Great shopping location. EXPENSIVE.

HAFEN HAMBURG (Seewartenstrasse 9; 11130) A former sailors' residence, this is located right on the port: picturesque, if not super-central. A good bargain, though. MODERATE.

MARITIM REICHSHOF (Kirchenallee 34; 248330) Classic old German hotel with prime St. Georg location. A good buy for the price. MODERATE.

HOTEL MONOPOL (Reeperbarhn 48/52) Decent touristic hotel, most notable for its central St. Pauli location. MODERATE.

SCHANZENSTERN (Schanzenstrasse 101; 433389) Inexpensive small hotel called "best cheapie" by the Tourist Board; not far from St. Pauli. INEXPENSIVE.

GAY HOTELS

The following hostelries are either gay-operated or extremely gay-friendly:

HOTEL ADLER (Ernst-Merck-Strasse 10) Decent, small gay hotel. INEXPENSIVE.

HOTEL VILLAGE (Steindamm 4) Nice little gay hotel in downtown area. INEXPENSIVE.

SARAH PETERSEN (Lange Reihe 50) Artsy/gay crowd. Way cool and right in St. Pauli. INEXPENSIVE.

RESTAURANTS

ABENDMAHL (Hein-Koeelisch Platz 6)
Post-modern decor, "in" crowd; excellent, innovative cuisine in St. Pauli.

ABTEI (in Hotel Abtei Abteistrasse 14)
Tiny, rather sedate restaurant that offers excellent French and German food. Out of the way, but a nice, semi-staid diversion.

ALSTERPAVILION (Jungfernsteig 54)
> Lovely spot on the Inner Alster. Food is unspec-
> tacular—bad, even—but a salad supports the gor-
> geous view.

ANNA E SEBASTIANO (Lehnweg 30)
> Expensive, fabulous Italian place hailed as one of
> Hamburg's best. Expense account helps.

BRUECKE (Innocentiastrasse 82)
> Chic-monied crowd, nouvelle German cuisine.
> Hamburg's best and brightest.

CAFÉ FEES (Holstenwall 34)
> In museum of Hamburg history. Best after 9:00
> P.M., but open all day. Artsy, scenic crowd, light
> Continental cuisine.

LE CANARD (Elbchaussee 139)
> Generally acknowledged to be the best in town.
> *Haute cuisine française,* gorgeous river view. Incred-
> ibly expensive.

ERICKA'S ECK (Sternstrasse 98)
> In the slaughterhouse district (Morrissey fans
> need not apply), this spot doesn't open till 3:00
> P.M.—clubbers, night trash galore. A decadent,
> messy must!

EISENSTEIN (Friedersallee 9)

Part of trendy film complex in Altona; situated in former ship factory. Hamburg's best pizza. Quite a scene.

JENA PARADIS (Klosterwall 23)

Named after an unidyllic East German city—thus an irony of name. Designed by Werner Buettner, a famed local *artiste*. Super-trendy; don't miss.

MARINEHOF (Admiralitaetstrasse 77)

Across the way from the Rialto; similarly tony crowd, Italian fare.

NIL (Neuer Pferdemarkt 5)

Former shoe store offers simple yet well-prepared food and nice design. Recommended.

RIALTO BAR (Michaelisbruecke 3)

Nouvelle Italian—sushi, yet. Oh-so-trendy upscale crowd.

RIVE (Van-der-Suissen Strasse 1)

The 40–deutschemark four-course dinner is the best deal in town—and in a super-trendy joint, a former ferry terminal with river views. Fab decor and crowd.

OESTERREICH (Martinstrasse 11)

Upscale Austrian in tony Eppendorf. Not avantgarde!

SAGRES (Vorsetzen 42)
Delish, unpretentious Portuguese eatery right by the harbor. Always busy with those in the know.

SCHOENBERGER (Grosse Freiheit 70)
Journalists, ad people, Continental cuisine in St. Pauli trendspot.

TAFELHAUS (Am Holstenkamp 71)
Yuppies have bestowed their favor on this Dutch-German cookery. Not cheap.

VIENNA (Fettstrasse 2)
Bistrot with fashionable Hamburg crowd.

(The cafés in Hamburg are a big part of the gay scene. You'll find café listings in the "Gay" section.)

SHOPPING

Hamburg's "city" area is a nonstop labyrinth of indoor arcades than run, roughly, between Moencke-bergstrasse and Gaensemarkt. These *Passage* can be everything from ultra-modern in design to the Old World extravagance of the Mellin-Passage. Generally speaking, the arcades and shopping streets become more expensive as one heads west, and cheaper in the vicinity of the train station. Spitalerstrasse, impossible to avoid, is a pedestrian street in the middle of this shopping chaos. Be sure not to miss Neuer Wall and

Grosse Bleichen, running along a lovely canal; both are lined with restaurants and cafés full of tony types.

Two residential areas that merit a casual stroll are Eppendorf (where stores slant avant-garde) and Poeseldorf (for more designer-ish goods).

GAY-ST. GEORG

CAFÉS

CAFÉ DES ARTISTES (Schwilinksystrasse 19)
New hotspot that's especially busy in late afternoon and early evenings. Young, attractive crowd.

CAFÉ GNOSA (Lange Reihe 93)
The real McCoy: One of the best gay cafés in the world. Cozy and friendly, with delicious, reasonably priced food and trendy, quasi-intellectual crowd. Not to be missed!

CAFÉ SPUND (Mohlenhofstrasse 3)
Less "in" than Gnosa, but worth a quick look-see.

CAFÉ UHRLAUB (Lange Reihe 63)
Traditional German *kneipe* cum café; older, less tony crowd than the others.

BARS

BLACK (Danziger Strasse 21)
 Leather buddies.

CHAPS (Woltmanstrasse 24)
 Ditto.

FIRST (Schauenburger Strasse 40)
 Working-class bar; not cool.

IM FRANZ (Steindamm 37)
 Older men congregate here.

MEZZO (Hoppel 3)
 Somewhat popular, mixed ages; not trendy.

TOM'S (Pulversteich 17)
 Leather dudes.

TUSCULUM (Kreuzweg 6)
 Average, uncool bar.

YELLOW (Pulverteich 17)
 OK bar.

BEL AMI, EXTRATOUR, and **TROCADERO,** all on the Zimmerpforte, are trashy hustler bars absorbing the overflow from the Central Station. (Just so you know.)

Dance Clubs

PIT CLUB (Pulverteich 17)
   Thai TVs on parade. A trashy hoot.

Gay-St. Pauli

Bars

ANGIE'S NIGHTCLUB (Spielbudenplatz 28)
   Mixed, OK nightspot. Nothing great.

CAP ARCONA (Taubenstrasse 23)
   Trash for cash.

CRAZY HORSE (Hein-Hoyer Strasse 62)
   Semi-trashy, untrendy St. Pauli bar.

DU AND ICH (Seilerstrasse 38a)
   Trashy rent boy joint.

FLAMINGO (Kastanienallee 33)
   Rent boys (again!).

FUNDUS (Detlev-Bremer Strasse 54)
   Older, cloney crowd.

LORELEY (Detlev-Bremer Strasse 44)
Small, unhip transvestite bar.

MONTE CHRISTO (Kastanienallee 7)
Pay to play.

PICCADILLY (Silberbacktwiete 1)
Cozy bar with older crowd.

PARADISO (Detlev-Bremer Strasse 50)
Working-class crowd; shows on weekends.

TOOM PEERSTALL-KATHARINA (Clemens-Schulz Strasse 44)
Katharina is Hamburg's reigning drag mama; she rules over this semi-trendy little spot, the best place to go in Hamburg.

WUNDERBAR (Talstrasse 14)
All types of guys; busy bar with hot jukebox.

DANCE CLUBS

CAMELOT (Hamburger Berg 13)
Cool house music party Fridays only: mixed, groovy crowd.

OPERA HOUSE (in Gruenspan, Grosse Freiheit 68)
Thursdays: cool gay dance night. 2nd Sunday: Love Ball, the trendiest (mixed) party in Hamburg. Love 'ya!

SPUNDLOCH (Paulinerstrasse 19)
Hamburg's oldest bar. Nothin' special.

GAY-BEYOND

CAFÉS

CAFÉ MISTRAL (Lehmweg 29)
Groovy, French-style café with outdoor seating and cool gay crowd. Not central, but worth a slight detour.

CAFÉ MAGNUS (Borgweg 8)
Well-known gay café, also rather far from the thick of things, but nice if you're in the nabe.

DANCE CLUBS

FRONT (Heidenkampsweg)
Nice little dance place; mixed and no longer trendy, but still attracts a decent gay crowd on nights nothing else is doing.

SAUNAS

APOLLO (Max-Brauer-Allee 277)
MELIDISSA (Max-Brauer-Allee 155)
SCHWITZKASTEN (Virchowstrasse 12–14)

Munich

Compared to the bug-up-their-ass attitude of most of Germany, Munich is a breath of fresh Alpine air. The Bavarian capital is indeed the land of dirndls and lederhosen—but it's also ever so much more.

Indeed, while it has within Germany a reputation for being hopelessly bourgeois, Munich is actually a sophisticated, nearly world-class town. Its cultural offerings are wide and deep (excuse the slightly smutty pun), its restaurant scene hip, and its nightlife diverse enough to keep you interested for as long you stay.

Also in the city's favor: Munich has a southern, relaxed feel; there's nothing here as dizzying as in Hamburg or Berlin. But nobody ever said taking it easy was a crime—well, certain Puritans maybe. My prescription for Munich fun: Slow down, amble around, and enjoy the ride.

More than anything, Munich has a look and feel all its own. Though much of the city was bombed during the war, the rebuilding was swift and sure; today, Munich has been restored to its former, glowing self. The Bavarian architecture is warm and winning; here, *Gemuetlichkeit* reigns. Everywhere, the city is dotted with inviting cafés and lush, green squares; it's the kind of place with which it's very easy to fall in love.

The other thing to remember is that Munich is a speedy train ride away from Salzburg, a perfect gem of a town. (A day trip or overnight, even, is an absolute must-do.) But so is Munich, a grand old city you just won't want to miss.

HOTELS

VIER JAHRESZEITEN (Maximilianstrasse 17; 230390) The grandest dame in town, right on Munich's most remarkable square. Classic German elegance at its best. VERY EXPENSIVE.

CONTINENTAL ROYAL CLASSIC (Max-Joseph-Strasse 5; 55157) In the center of Munich's antiques district, this is a fabulously designed old gem. Recommended. EXPENSIVE.

KONIGSHOF (Karlsplatz 25; 551360) Gorgeous oldster that's both central and very nice. EXPENSIVE.

OPERA (St-Anna-Strasse 10; 225533) Charming, very discreet hotel, a preferred address for people in the know. EXPENSIVE.

ENGLISCHER GARTEN (Liebergesellstrasse 8; 392034) Breathtaking location—a rustic guest house in town. Absolutely unique. MODERATE.

HOTEL BITTMANN (Pullacherstrasse 24; 797083) Groovy, modern designer hotel, home to artsy and fashion types. Cool! MODERATE.

HOTEL SPLENDID (Maximilianstrasse 54; 296606) Quietly elegant old charmer; good location, too. Recommended. MODERATE.

LUITPOLD (Schützenstrasse 14; 594461) Rustic, woodsy rooms are winners. Nice! MODERATE.

THERESIA (Luisenstrasse 51; 52150) Cheap, decent place to stay in arty Schwabing. Recommended. INEXPENSIVE.

PENSION BECK (Thierstchstrasse 36; 225768) Very basic, very cheap pension. You get wha'cha pay for . . . INEXPENSIVE.

PENSION ASTA (Seidlstrasse 2A; 592515) Cheap little pension—some charm, even—near the railway station. INEXPENSIVE.

RESTAURANTS

BAMBERGER HAUS (Brunnerstrasse 2)
Lovely baroque house with very nice menu at 18 DM. A perennial favorite among locals.

BRASSERIE BUNUEL in Arabilla Hotel (Arabellas-trasse 5)
>   Perhaps the best French kitchen in town. Very "in" indeed. Reserve early.

LA BUCA (Koeniniginstrasse 34)
>   Upscale-chic Italian place with (successful) artists, etc. You know the crowd.

LISSABON BAR (Breisacher Strasse 22)
>   Groovy joint with fags, artists, students, etc. Quite lively!

NIAWARAN (Innere Wiener Strasse 18)
>   Gorgeous, vaulted ceilings and Persian/Afghani cuisine. Very special indeed.

NITAYA (Villa Borghese Nitaya, Lehel Thierstrasse 35)
>   Munich's best Thai restaurant, rather more up-scale than you'd think. Nice.

RUE DES HALLES (Heithausen Steinstrasse 18)
>   Trendy, quasi-Nouvelle French eatery, very chichi just now.

SABITZER (Reitunovstrasse, 21)
>   Postmodern decor, chichi crowd, and Nouvelle cuisine are this place's hallmarks.

SPATENHAUS (Rezidenzstrasse 12)
Hearty Southern German fare and charming country decor. Come hungry!

TANTRIS (Johann-Frichte-Strasse, 7)
Regarded as Munich's most innovative Nouvelle kitchen. *Très cher* and chic.

WEISSES BRAEUHAUS (Tal, 10)
Really touristy, but a fine place to sample stick-to-the-ribs Bavarian cooking.

SHOPPING

Munich's most upscale shops can be found on the Maximilianstrasse and its environs. But remember . . . Munich is not really known as a fashion city, and the usual roundup of international names is bound to cost you more here than at home.

Instead, amble around Hans-Sachs-Strasse, the street that houses many of the gay bars. Here you'll find groovy clothing stores, gay specialty stores, and the like. Muellerstrasse also contains stores of interest to gays.

Alternative and artsy types will not want to miss the Schwabing district, rather like New York's East Village (if much more upscale and less dilapidated). Here, the main drags are Baerstrasse, Arcistrasse, and Schellingstrasse.

But take my advice, and don't try to make shopping your main focus here (unless you're inexplicably into Bavarian artifacts and curious). Instead, chew up the scenery and explore Munich's touristic sites; save your greenbacks for Hamburg, London, or Paree.

GAY

BARS

BELL (Utzschneiderstrasse 4)
Modern bar cum café with food. Just OK.

BOTT (Blumenstrasse 15)
Leather/jeans bar; fairly popular among that crowd.

JUICE (Buttermelcherstrasse 22)
Bar/restaurant with casual crowd; best early evenings.

LOEWENGRUBE (Reisingerstrasse 5)
Leather/western place.

MARGO (Reichenbachstrasse 21)
Open from early evening on; café with food, mixed ages.

MORIZZ (Klenzenstrasse 43)
Currently, the best and semi-trendiest place in town, with cute, young crowd. Small restaurant with international fare; clublike bar gets going later on. A must, especially on weekends.

NIL (Hans-Sachs-Strasse 2)
Very busy watering hole with something-for-every-one clientele: yuppies, mature men, punks. Open from early evening; a good place to start the night.

PILS-STUBEN 2000 (Dultstrasse 1)
One of Munich's oldest gay bars, still popular for average Joes. Trendies need not apply.

TEDDY BAR (Hans-Sachs-Strasse 1)
Tepid leather influence, older crowd; across the street from Nil.

TONIGHT (Detmoldstrasse 2)
Young crowd, sometimes trendy. Best late.

Dance Clubs

EMPIRE (Thalkirchner Strasse 2)
Mixed gay/lesbian. OK, nothing special.

NEW YORK (Sonnenstrasse 25)
Munich's busiest dance bar, lately on a techno craze. Fairly seventies in decor, though. Best after 11:00 P.M. and weekends.

TOGETHER AGAIN (Muellerstrasse 1)
Dance club cum drag shows. Less than inspiring, but worth a look-see.

SAUNAS

NEUE CITY SAUNA (Westermuehlstrasse 8)

ITALY

Florence

Florence, my dears, is a pearl.

Slightly less so, of course, during tourist season, when the town is overrun by hordes of Japanese in package tours. Then, the crowds are so thick that even circulating in the city can be a chore. So take my advice and go off-season; April or October are excellent bets.

Whenever you go, be prepared for an aesthetic experience that's second to none: Between its art treasures and fashion preeminence, Florence has flair that never ends. Plus, its natural setting on the Arno River makes it one of the most picturesque cities in the world.

But know this: Florence is basically a small town. Unlike what they tell you in other guidebooks, you really can see everything in a couple of days (unless, of course, you're writing your Ph.D. dissertation in art history). For as much as Florence has to offer, it's not a city that tries to trap you into extended stays. Its *piazze* (unlike Rome's) are generally not bordered by inviting cafés, at least not during the day; people always seem to be hustling from shops to galleries and back. So once you run out of things to do, you can't really just hang around for days on end.

The city has two good gay nightspots, though neither gets started till midnight, raising the question of what one does in the interim hours from dinner until then. If you're like the natives, you'll simply amble about on the main drags—a variation on the theme of lemmings to the sea—which are the via por Santa Maria to the Ponte Vecchio, then back up the Piazza della Repubblica; but this perambulating can get tired fast. Odd that there aren't the café society or pop-culture doings a city like this should have. One mixed place, the Cardillac (sic) is trying to fill the gap with performance and such, but thus far hasn't been able to draw much of a crowd. (Old habits die hard.)

Are Florentine men the most gorgeous in the world? It's just possible, and you may want to make meeting one high on your list. Doing so in the clubs or in the city's one sauna is certainly possible, though gays here tend to travel in packs, and tearing them away from their fellow wolves can be major work.

So don't sweat it—enjoy Florence's many charms and hope you get lucky. After all, that's the best strategy anywhere you go . . .

HOTELS

SAVOY (Piazza della Repubblica, 7; 283313) Perhaps the plushest game in town. Very grand, gorgeously appointed, and the location can't be beat. VERY EXPENSIVE.

EXCELSIOR (Piazza Ognissanti, 3; 264201) Right on the Arno, an elegant member of the CIGA chain. Fabulous views and service. EXPENSIVE.

HELVETIA & BRISTOL (Via dei Pescioni; 2; 287814) Century-old marvel that's amazingly furnished, with different style for each floor. Really lovely. EXPENSIVE.

VILLA MEDICI (Via del Prato, 42) Elegant and grand, nicely located. Locals love the place. EXPENSIVE.

ALBANI (Via Fiume, 12; 211045) Brand hew hotel with classically Florentine room decor—a cut above others in its class. A bit off the beaten path, but not too far. EXPENSIVE.

MONA LISA (Borso Pinti, 27; 2429751) Italian classic style in an old charmer. MODERATE.

LOGGIATO DEL SERVITTI (Piazza Annunziata, 3; 219165) Fab old palazzo, all for a song. Nice! MODERATE.

MACHIAVELLI PALACE (Via Nazionale, 10; 2360008) Utterly charming, medium-priced hotel, some rooms with views and balconies. Recommended. MODERATE.

HOTEL BONCIANI (Via Panzani, 17; 2382341) Tourist class hotel that's not without some charm. Good location. MODERATE.

PORTA ROSSA (Via Porta Rossa, 19; 287551) Florence's oldest hotel, former home to Stendhal and Balza. Charming, if somewhat tattered, and cheap. Recommended. INEXPENSIVE.

LA RESIDENZA (Via Tornabuoni, 8; 284197) Tiny hostelry overlooking the Arno, a great budget option. INEXPENSIVE.

HOTEL MEDICI (Via de Medici, 6; 284818) Nice little place that's very gay-friendly. Recommended. INEXPENSIVE.

RESTAURANTS

AL LUME DI CANDELA (Via delle Terme, 23r)
   Wonderful Tuscan food in a marvelous medieval edifice. Lovely decor, too. Recommended.

CAFFE CONCERTO (Lungarno Cristoforo Colombo)
   Perhaps Florence's most romantic dining spot. Lovely terrace, too.

CAMMILLO (Borgo Sant' Jacopo, 57)
   Good prices, great food, in this quasi-fashionable trattoria, favored by Fiorentines.

CANTINA BARBAGIANNI (Via Sant'Egidio, 13r)
   Florentine/international kitchen that's very much in vogue just now. A favorite among locals—and that's saying a lot.

CANTINETTI ANTINORI (Piazza Antinori 3)
   Trendy little cantina with fabulous light fare. The perfect place for a summer day's lunch.

CIBREO (Via del Macci, 118r)
Unpretentious little restaurant with recipes from Florence and beyond. Very much a local scene.

COCO LEZZONE (Via del Parioncino, 26r)
Simply fabulous Florentine food. Very popular indeed, and rightly so.

ENOTECA PINCHIORRI (Via Ghibellina, 87)
Often cited as Florence's best. Franco-Italian specialties, grand spectacle, endless wine list. Enormously expensive. A splurge to be reckoned with.

GARGA (Via del Moro, 50/52)
Very "in" place with whimsically decorated room. Innovative cooking, too. Chichi.

GAUGUIN (Via degli Alfani, 24r)
Vegetarian joint with young, gay-friendly staff and clientele.

IL LATINI (Via Palchetti, 6r)
"Stick-to-the-ribs" food at reasonable prices. Unpretentious surroundings; but the food's the thing here.

LE CAVE (Via della Cave, 16 Maiano/Fiesole)
Lovely spot just outside Florence that's pure magic—Tuscan cooking at its best. Ask your concierge about the bus to Fiesole—it's easy—or cab it out. Nice!

LE FONTICINE (Via Nazionale, 76r)
Excellent trattoria with fine Florentine food. Highly recommended.

MONKEY BUSINESS (Pizza della Signoria, 1)
Yuppie-trendy restaurant that attracts Florence's young upscale (cum business) crowd. If it's your bag.

OLIVEIRO (Via Delle Terme, 51r)
Tuscan cuisine, lovely setting, and very "in" crowd. Go.

OSTERIA No. 1 (Via delle Oche, 12–16r)
Slightly touristy but nonetheless excellent trattoria. Case the crowd and decide.

SABATINI (Via Panzani, 9a)
Rather less well regarded than in its halcyon days, this is still a famous, if somewhat staid eatery. Your choice . . .

SHOPPING

Make no mistake: Florence's shopping is the best in the world. Fashion is everything here, and as far as I'm concerned, the natives are better turned out than in Rome or Milan. (I don't know anywhere except Paris where straight men look so fucking good.)

Where shall I send you? The point is moot; the whole damn city's a shopping arcade. Most upscale is via Tornabuoni, home to all the expected high fashion names (Versace reigns here); via della Vigna Nuova (Armani's shop is here); via Porto Rosso, via por Santa Maria, and via Roma are other major shopping arteries.

But that's just a start. Florence is a small place, easily traversed by foot, and you'll discover your favorite places, be they classic or avant-garde. And, oh, that American Express card—don't leave home without it. You'll regret it if you do.

GAY

BARS

CARDILLAC (Via Alfani, 57r)
Trendy mixed bar/café. Not a gay bar, but a new meeting point for Florence's artsy types—performances, readings, and such. Slow to take off—it's often empty—but who knows?

CRISCO CLUB (Via San Egidio, 43r)
Very popular, cruisy bar with busy downstairs backroom. The sexiest name in town. Closed Tuesdays. A must!

DANCE CLUB

TABASCO (Piazza Santa Cecilia, 3)
Italy's first gay dance club, it's still going strong.

Closed Monday; most packed on weekends. Subdued by Paris or New York standards, it's still a hotspot in Italian terms. (Note: Though right in the center of town, this place is murder to find. It's on the southwest end of the Piazza Signoria, behind a bar/café; the Piazza Santa Cecilia is no more than a back alley, not found on most maps. Walking north on the Via por Santa Maria, turn right into the Piazza Signoria, then hang another left when you see the bar, into Santa Cecilia.)

SAUNA

FLORENCE BATHS (Via Guelfa, 93r)

Milan

Milan presents a quandary. Though hardly a touristic mecca, it is undoubtedly Italy's most diversified center of gay life. Therefore . . . shouldst thou visit or not?

It depends. (How's that for a waffle?) Chances are, you're either in Milan on business—fashion or finance—or just passing through. In the former case, your schedule is predetermined; in the latter, the choice is up to you. By all means, make the stop—but I'm here to tell you to give it a day and a half, tops.

Truth is, Milan just isn't an embracing city; an apropos motto would be "Do your business and leave." There are few grand cafés that beckon the visitor to linger; the most austere of piazzas; and precious little public green space. The architecture is undistinguished, the general aura bleak: no Circe of cities, Milan.

Rather, the city's appeal lies in its unforeseen charms, the whirl of its showrooms and studios, and in the chichi restaurants of the day. (All are listed here, of course.) Admittedly, Milan's business world is of no interest to the tourist, so after you've seen The Last Supper and the Duomo, you may well be tempted to hit the road.

However and whyever you're in town, Milan boasts (for Italy) an impressive array of gay loci—some downright sexy. Be forewarned, though: The unintrepid need not apply. First, opening days and times are whimsical at best, in utter disregard to "official" opening schedules. As a rule, Mondays and Tuesdays are always out, and—with the exception of After Line—clubs don't even begin to roll till midnight, later on weekends. Plus, many of the bars are outside the range of the Metro, necessitating travel via bus or train, whose routes can best be described as Italianate (read: labyrinthine and abstruse). Finally, several of these places are hidden on the outskirts of Milan, and that can mean a $15 cab ride home (at least—Italian cabbies are notoriously unscrupulous). Which is to ask: How much will you put up with to get laid?

The bottom line: If you're here on business, make the most of it. Vacationers, give up a day or two, then move on to Florence, Rome, and points beyond.

HOTELS

EXCELSIOR (Piazza Duca D'Aosta, 9; 6785) Grand old hotel that puts you in a real Italianate mood. Lovely and majestic. VERY EXPENSIVE.

HOTEL REGINA (Via C. Correnti, 13; 581 06913) Fabulous Old World charmer right on a great shopping street. EXPENSIVE.

PIERRE MILANO (Via de Amicis, 32; 805 6221) New property for business execs, a forty-seven-room-place that's a ten-minute walk from the Duomo. EXPENSIVE.

PRINCIPE DI SAVOIA (Piazza della Repubblica, 17; 6230) Traditional Italian elegance, recently renovated to its original splendor. Highly recommended. EXPENSIVE.

GRAN DUCA DE YORK (Via Moneta, 1; 874863) Ascetic elegance in an almost monastical old palace that's really unique. Odd and endearing. MODERATE.

JOLLY PRESIDENT (Largo Augusto, 10; 7746) The best-priced hotel near the Duomo. Central if uncharming. MODERATE.

ANTICA LOCANDA SOLFERINO (Via Castelfidardo, 2; 6570129) Lovely old palace in artsy Brera nabe. Really nice, and a comparative bargain, too. INEXPENSIVE.

LONDON HOTEL (Via Rovello, 3; 720 20 166) Very central, home to many modeling hopefuls. Not gorgeous, but a great value. Recommended. INEXPENSIVE.

RESTAURANTS

AL GARBALDI (Visle Monte Grappa, 7)
Superchic Milanese eatery where fashionites teem.

BAGUTTA (Via Bagutta, 14)
Not as "in" as before, but still a very popular place. A longtime favorite that's sure to please; food, Italian.

BICE (Via Borgospesso, 12)
> The chicest joint in town, and keystone of the international "chain." Very "in."

BIFE SCALA (Piazza della Scala)
> Upscale chic, memorable Italian food.

BRICIOLA (Via Solferino, 25)
> Fabulous food, supermodels galore. Milan's finest dine here.

CAFE INDIA (Via Petrella, 19)
> Ultra-trendy Italo-Indian (yes!) cuisine and artsy clientele. Sunday brunch a definite "in" scene.

DIXIELAND (Via Quadrio, 9)
> Egads! Tex-Mex has hit Italia. And Milan's young scenesters lap it up.

GIANNINO (Via Armatore Sciesa, 8)
> Long noted as one of Milan's top restaurants. Very expensive, but worth the splurge. Not trendy, just a gastronomic gem.

LA RANARITA (Via Fatabenefratelli, 2)
> Trendy fashionites abound. Noisy, busy, and much fun.

LA TAGLIATTA (Via Ariberto, 1)
> Wonderful trattoria where you'll eat very well. Recommended.

LE LANGHE (Corso Como, 6)
  Excellent trattoria that's always full with a trendy fashion crowd. Recommended.

MOON FISH (Via Bagutta, 2)
  More pricey sister to Paper Moon; really excellent fish fare. Recommended.

ST. ANDREW'S (Via St. Andrew's, 23)
  Top designers—Armani, Ferre, etc.—and their acolytes hold court here. Clublike atmosphere and fabulous food.

SAVINI (Galleria Vittoria Emmanuele, 2)
  Italian fare, still popular after all these years. Formality reigns, but with not too heavy a hand.

SOLFERINO (Via Castelfidaro, 2)
  Very comfortable, almost rustic restaurant that's a good bargain, too. Great food, sometimes glittering crowd.

TRATTORIA AURORA (Via Savona, 23)
  Lovely country decor, Piemontese kitchen. Very unpretentious and friendly; utterly untouristy.

SHOPPING

Here, I must differ from the general perception of Milan as a shopping paradise. True, there are good shops, and yes, the fashion industry is based here; but there just isn't the magic of Florence here. This has more to do with the charm of the respective cities than the shops themselves, but it's not unrelated to the general shopping ambience.

Via Monte Napoleone is typically cited as the key street in town, though it's home to top designers and high-priced goods (especially slanted toward women), rather than anything trendy or avant-garde. Via Torino is a winding street that has casual, popular-priced goods, as does Via C. Correnti, which it becomes. Also, try the Galleria Vittorio Emmanuele II and surrounding streets, which are also devoted to less-expensive goods.

But really, take my advice: Save your money and save your energy for Florence. Shopping there is a joy of joys; doing so here is going through the motions.

GAY

BARS

AFTER LINE (Via Sammartini, 25)
Large, two-room bar near central station. Cute young crowd; open from early evening. More convivial than cruisy.

ALEXANDER'S BAR (Via Pindaro, 23)
Cruisy bar that opens after midnight and stays open till the morning hours. Backroom, too. Hot!

COMPANY (Via Benadir, 14)
Leather/fetishist bar. Membership only; talk your way in (maybe).

ONE WAY BAR (Via Renzo e Lucia, 3)
Sexy bar with backroom, open till 6:00 A.M. on weekends. Recommended!

QUERELLE (Via de Castille, 20)
Clique-y club under auspices of Arco (Italian gay group). Again, try to talk your way in, but no promises . . .

DANCE CLUBS

HD (Via Tajani, 11)
Small disco, best on weekends. Just OK.

KILLER PLASTICO (Via Umbria, 120)
Famous alternative music club now has a fab gay night—Thursdays only!

MACHO MAN (Via Boscovich, 48)
Leather crowd at play.

NUOVA IDEA (Via de la Castilia, 30)
A legend. Two huge dance rooms: one for polka/waltzes (a hoot!), the other for disco dancin'. Like nowhere else in the world . . .

ZIP CLUB (Corso Sempione, 76)
>   Multi-use complex: sauna, dancing, bar, etc. Quite
>   a scene. Go very late on weekends.

SAUNAS (Usual open times: noon to midnight)

ALEXANDER'S (Via Pindaro, 23)
MAGIC SAUNA (Via Maiocchi, 8)
ONE WAY SAUNA (Via Renzo e Lucia, 3)
THERMAS (Via Bezzecca, 9)

Rome

Rome is a capital without a cause.

Look at it this way: Italy's fashion center is Milan; its art center, Florence. The country's political system resides in Rome, yes—though it's so splintered and divisive that it hardly counts at all. (And, as any student of history knows, Italians only pay attention to government when they absolutely have to.)

Besides, when's the last time you opened the paper and read about goings-on in Rome? (Those people wearing $500 sunglasses and waving French cigarettes in the back pages of *Vogue* and *Interview* are all in Milan.) Unless you remember *La Dolce Vita* days—and who'd admit to it?—Rome hasn't really been a part of our collective modern consciousness. Plus, since the demise of Franco, it's Madrid that has captured the crown in the dusty-old-capitals-turning-chic category, don't you think?

But Romans have never much cared what the rest of the world thinks. Today they still lumber along in that messy, chaotic, life-loving way that's theirs alone. In Milan (the Switzerland of Italy), everything works; in Rome, nothing does, and there's no reason why it should. It just might spoil all the fun.

There's plenty to do in Rome, especially if you're the archaeological or hyper-religious type. But far more fun than schlepping from place to place is simply to fall into the city's drowsy-liquid-gorgeous pace and march happily, sexily along. Trip down the streets of Trastevere, fight with the waiter in your squareside café, fall in love. It's the crazy mix of romance and contretemps that makes Rome the city of everyone's dreams.

HOTELS

MAJESTIC (Via Veneto, 50; 48641) Stars galore have graced this classic hostelry—incredibly luxe and spectacular. Recommended. VERY EXPENSIVE.

HOTEL DE LA VILLE (Via Sistine, 67; 67331) Lovely old place with gorgeous terraces and views, plus fabulous furnishings. Very Roman indeed. VERY EXPENSIVE.

RAPHAEL (Large Febo, 2; 68 28 31) Gorgeous residence near the Piazza Navona, less stuffy and formalistic than the places listed above. EXPENSIVE.

ALBERGO D'INGHILTERRA (Via Boccadi Leone, 14; 672161) Nineteenth-century marvel, a former home to Hemingway. Ask for a room with a city view terrace. Fabulous! EXPENSIVE.

COLUMBUS (Via della Concilizone, 33; 686487) A grand old palace near St. Peter's houses this opulent hotel. Very Old Italy! EXPENSIVE.

FONTANA (Piazza di Trevi, 96; 6786113) Monastic property near the Trevi Fountain; rather austere, yet a good bargain and great price. MODERATE.

SCALINATA DI SPAGNA (Piazza Trinita dei Monti, 17; 6 79 30 06) Really Roman, a charming oldster that's especially nice. Recommended. MODERATE.

ALBERGO DEL SOLA AL PANTHEON (Piazza della Rotonda, 63; 6 78 04) Gorgeous, classic place with views of the Pantheon. Erstwhile, a literati crowd. MODERATE.

ALBERGO DEI PORTOGHESE (Via dei Portoghese, 1; 6 86 42 31) Famous pension that Americans have loved for years. Somewhat overpriced, yet still recommended for its location and relative value. MODERATE.

ALBERGO DEL SOLE (Via del Biscione, 76; 6880 6873) Nice pension that's perfect for budgeteers. Recommended. INEXPENSIVE.

ALBERGO ABRUZZI (Piazza della Rotonda, 69; 6 79 20 21) Good little hotel near the Pantheon that's an exceptional bargain and well located to boot. INEXPENSIVE.

PENSIONE SAN ANDREA (Via XX Settembre, 89; 4814775) Very basic—and very cheap—*pensione* near the train station. For super-budgeteers only! INEXPENSIVE.

DINESEN (Via Di Porta Pinciana, 18; 460932) One of Rome's loveliest inexpensive places, near the Via Veneto. Quite atmospheric. INEXPENSIVE.

RESTAURANTS

ALBERTO CIARLE (Piazza San Cosimato, 40)
Expensive, but worth it. Known as the best place to eat fish in Rome. On the elegant side.

AUGUSTO E SANDRO (Piazza di Renzi, 15)
Celebrity-soaked trattoria and wonderful Roman specialties. Go!

BIONDO TEVERE (Via Ostiense, 178)
A classic romantic place with views of the Tevere River.

CHECCO ER CARETTIERE (Via Benedetti, 10)
Friendly Trastevere place with to-die-for food and crowd. Highly recommended.

DUE L'ADRONIA (Piazza Nicosia, 24)
Very chic restaurant, home to Italian film stars galore. See and be seen!

FIERA MOSCA (Piazza de Mercanti)
The surreal decor is reason alone for seeing this place. The food is another.

GINO E PIETRO (Via del Governo Vecchio, 106)
A good trattoria that Romans applaud for its value and food. You will, too.

LA TAVOLE DI MARMO (Via Trastevere, 53)
Lovely pizzeria in Trastevere that's a great value, with great food.

ROMOLO (Via di Porta Settimiana, 8)
On everyone's best-of list, an ages-old Trastevere eatery; nothing's more Roman. Lovely.

QUINZI E GABRIELLI (Via della Coppelle, 5)
Trendy eatery with Italy's version of nouvelle cuisine.

VECCHIA ROMA (Piazza Campitelli)
A classic restaurant on a lovely square with traditional recipes, wonderfully presented and prepared. A local favorite.

SHOPPING

In all the years I've gone there, I don't think I've ever bought anything to wear in Rome. That's probably because I never go to Italy without visiting Florence, where shopping is both more chic and serene. Rome's scope of merchandise seems to cover the kind of expensive "designer" merchandise oil sheiks buy and jeans-y stuff, with no visible niche for the urban avant-garde. But if you must . . .

The area around the Spanish Steps is ostensibly Rome's most elegant shopping area, though it houses the kind of merchandise I abjured above. Key streets here are Via Borgognona and Via Condotti—rather like New York's Fifth Avenue, full of tourists and rich locals with limited taste.

Far more interesting is the Via del Corso, where stores slant youngward and more casual. It's where trendy—and would-be—Romans shop. Via Frattina is another street that attracts a varied clientele and offers shops of interest in all price brackets.

For local color and less tourists, you might want to stroll down the Via Ottaviano and Via Cola di Rienzo, which are near the Vatican. Even if you don't buy anything, you'll be seeing an interesting new side of Rome.

GAY

Traditionally, Rome's gay scene has been undercover and fairly turgid. While it still isn't Paris or Madrid, the scene has improved tangibly (though, one suspects, attitudes toward homosexuals are still unaccepting except in the most chichi or liberal/intellectual circles). In any case, at least there are now more than a couple of places to keep you amused during your stay.

BARS

APEIRON CLUB (Via dei Quattro Cantoni, 5)
American-style bar with backroom. Modern and fun!

CONTATTO (Via Gregoriana, 54)
Large video bar that's open till 4:00 A.M. New, and looks to be a smash. Beware of hustlers in nice boys' clothing.

HANGAR (Via in Selci, 69)
Casual, cruisy bar that gets very busy after 11:30 P.M. Recommended.

DANCE CLUBS

BLUE ZONE (Via Campania, 37)
Gay party on Monday nights only—when other places are closed. Trendy young crowd.

CASTELLO (Via Di Porta Castello 44)
Sexy gay party on Friday nights, very "in" right now.

L'ALIBI (Via di Monte Testaccio, 44)
Rome's oldest gay dance club, still going strong. Young, if not overly fashionable, crowd.

L'ANGELO AZZURRO (Via Cardina Merry del Val, 13)

One of Rome's oldest clubs, now fairly mixed, with heavy gay presence. Young-ish crowd. On its way down, methinks, as Rome discovers the newer Eurobars.

MAX'S (Via Achille Grandi, 7)

Bar/disco; all types congregate here. Closed Monday.

SAUNAS

APOLLION (Via Mecenate, 59)
TERME DI ROMA (Via Persio, 4)

THE
NETHERLANDS

Amsterdam

There are probably a million reasons you shouldn't quit your job and move to Amsterdam at once. Unfortunately, unless you're categorically opposed to gorgeous men, fabulous nightlife, and calm-inducing canals, I can't think of the first damn one. (Even RuPaul could learn to navigate a runway in wooden shoes!)

Falling in love with the Netherlands is, indeed, a very easy thing. From the moment you arrive at Schipol Airport, you know things are going to be great. Unlike Kennedy—where jetting in is rather like arriving at Bombay—Schipol fairly cries out, "First World." It's more than an airport; Schipol doubles as the largest duty-free shop in the world. (And believe me—there are real bargains to be had here, especially if cologne, ciggies, and booze are your thang.) Finding your luggage is idiot-proof, and your bags will probably be there before you are. Then, a sparkling Dutch train whisks you to Central Station in downtown Amsterdam for less than three bucks. (At JFK, you'd probably still be outside, damning the unpredictable Carey bus.)

Amsterdam means so many things to so many people—to gay travelers, especially—that I'd be the last one to tell you how you should feel. Certainly, the city's reputation as a gay mecca has stood for years; yet, given the relaxing of attitudes toward gays in most major cities of the Western world, this quality need not be considered Amsterdam's only calling card. By the same token, druggies can find pot and hash anywhere; those so interested hardly have to trek across the Atlantic to toke up. (Hard drugs are still highly illegal, and fines are probably greater than in the United States—caveat emptor!) In sum, erstwhile "aberrant" behavior, so long a reason to travel to Holland, can be flagrantly indulged in practically anywhere these days.

So come to Amsterdam for any other reason, and expect to be wowed: Few cities so instantly make the visitor feel at home. Whether it's the gentle nature of the Dutch or the soothing influence of the city's ubiquitous canals, you'll want to call Amsterdam "your town" in a flash. And why not? The city has beckoned the untolerated of the world for centuries; why shouldn't it take in crazy old you?

One of the nicest things about Amsterdam is how you can take in the city at your own pace and never feel guilty about taking it slow. Amsterdam is assuredly lively, yet it's never as suffocating as high-rise towns. Somehow, lazing around a café or taking a boat tour of the canals (unabashedly touristy, but major fun!) doesn't seem slothful at all. Of course, this kind of procrastination ("Oh, let's do the Rijksmuseum tomorrow") results in unintentionally prolonged stays; though once again I ask, "Why not?"

To be sure, Amsterdam offers oodles of touristic stuff to do. The city's range of museums is breathtaking: must-sees are the aforementioned Rijksmuseum (*mucho* Rembrandt, including "Night Watch," and other Dutch masters' work); the Stedjtmuseum (devoted to modern art); and the Van Gogh (pronounce Mister Earless as they do in Woody Allen films, and the Dutch will be very impressed!). But don't miss the fascinating Amsterdam Historical Museum and, of course, the Anne Frank House, devoted to the fostering of tolerance and humanism worldwide.

Alternately, spend your time just ambling about: Getting lost in Amsterdam is a stroller's dream. The city isn't tiny, but you can certainly cover its core (*centrum,* in Dutch) by foot. To traverse long distances, there is a hugely comprehensive system of streetcars that can take you anywhere you want to go. Admittedly, the sheer number of routes makes the tram map more than a little confusing, but Amsterdammers are always happy to help you on your way.

A firm believer in bodies at rest as well as in motion, I'm delighted to report that Amsterdam is a café sitter's nirvana. Under no circumstances should you miss De Kroon, a vast Old World café that's especially happening at night, or De Jahre, a large, airy, very contemporary spot. Two small gay coffeehouses, Downtown and the Other Side, are also nice places to hang out and read expensive foreign magazines.

One of the Netherlands' little-heralded touristic pluses is its compact, easily traveled size. If you're planning to spend more than a few days in Amsterdam, I heartily advise side trips to the delightful towns of Haarlem and Utrecht, neither more than an hour away from Amsterdam. Either city—or both!—provides a lovely taste of life in what is perhaps the kindest, gentlest country on Earth.

HOTELS

HÔTEL DE L'EUROPE (Nieuwe Doelenstraat 2–4; (800) 223-6800 or 623.4836) Belle Epoque grande dame for expense accounters. Lovely and right in the thick of things. VERY EXPENSIVE.

AMERICAN (Leidesplein 28; 623.4813) A landmark, part of Amsterdam's scenery for over a century. Not super-central, but trendy in an offbeat way. Don't miss its legendary bar/café. EXPENSIVE.

GRAND HOTEL KRASNAPOLSKY (Dam 9; 554.9111) Old World charm for days; very central. EXPENSIVE.

AMBASSADE (Herengracht 341; 626.2333) Charming old Dutch hotel in traditional canal house. Really lovely! MODERATE.

HOKSBERGEN (Singel 301; 626.6043) Great canal location, for a song. INEXPENSIVE.

KEIZERSHOF (Keizersgracht 618; 622.2855) Tiny but atmospheric Dutch pension; unique! INEXPENSIVE.

SINGEL (Singel 13; 626.3108) Modern rooms in a gorgeous old canal house—a real find. INEXPENSIVE.

GAY HOTELS

AMSTERDAM HOUSE (Staalkade 4; 626.25.77) Unique concept: apartments and houseboats; especially good for long stays. An interesting option for adventurous types. MODERATE.

HOTEL ORFEO (Leidsekruisstraat 14; 623.1347) Friendly, clean gay guest house. INEXPENSIVE.

HOTEL NEW YORK (Herengracht 13; 624.3066) Modern, smallish hotel. Central, if less than ultra-charming. INEXPENSIVE.

HOTEL ENGELAND (Roemer Visscherstraat 30; 612.9691) Quiet, charming little hotel. INEXPENSIVE.

THE WATERFRONT HOTEL (Singel 485; 625.5774) Absolutely recommended. Lovely little hotel right on Singel canal. INEXPENSIVE.

HOTEL UNIQUE (Kerkstraat 37; 624.4785) Basic, cheap gay hotel; very central.

ITC HOTEL (Prinsengracht 1051; 623.0230) Great choice in historical building, canalside. INEXPENSIVE.

RESTAURANTS

ARTUSI (Prinsengracht 999)
Semi-trendy Italian spot. Great food, upscale crowd.

BROODJE VAN KOOTJE (around town)
Very basic, but a great introduction to traditional Dutch sandwiches. Cheap.

CHRISTOPHE (Leliegracht 46)
Chic, Michelin-cited French haute cuisine; a hot ticket indeed.

DYNASTY (Regulierdwarstratt 30)
Chinese/Vietnamese/Thai fare in trendy setting. Hot and hip.

EXCELSIOR (Nieuwe Doelenstraat 2–4)
Classic French menu overlooking the Amstel River. Expensive but worth it.

GAUCHOS (Spuistratt 3)
Scrumptious Argentinian *churrasco*. Vegetarians need not apply.

HAESJE CLAES (N.Z. Voorburgival 320)
Great place to taste authentic Dutch food (not an easy order, believe it or not!).

LE GARAGE (Ruysdaelstratt 54)
The ne plus ultra of Amsterdam's scene. Very
trendy, very French, very good.

LE PECHEUR (Regulierdwarstratt 32)
Very "in," French-style fish. Chic and *cher*!

LUDEN (Spuistraat 304–308)
Really nice brasserie in gorgeous garden house.
Slightly, but not overbearingly, yuppie crowd.

PIER 10 (De Ruyterkade Steiger 10)
An Amsterdam favorite, serving world-class Continental fare at less-than-stratospheric prices.

RADEN MAS (Stadhkouderskaede 8)
A fine introduction to Indonesian cuisine, on the
upscale.

ROSA'S CANTINA (Regulierdwarstratt 38)
Informal, inexpensive Mexican place in Amsterdam's boystown. OK, but it ain't East L.A.!

SICHUAN (Regulierdwarstratt 35)
New Chinese eatery, soaking up the fashion crowd.

SLUIZER (Utrechtestratt 45)
Excellent, moderately priced fish menu that both
locals and tourists love; same-named meat restaurant next door. Nice garden, too.

TARTUFFO (Singel 449)
Trendy trattoria. Downstairs: casual. Upstairs: more formal scene.

TEMPO DOELOE (Utrechtestraat 75)
Casual, cheap, and spicy Indonesian place. Popular.

TOSCANINI (Goudsblogentraatt 52)
Basic Italian fare, well-prepared and quite reasonable. Opt for pastas.

TOWN HOUSE (Regulierdwarstratt 28)
Upscale-chic gem with French/Continental point of view. Hot!

CAFÉS

DE JAHREN (Nieuwe Doelenstraat 22)
The café of the moment. Large, luscious scene; very gay-friendly.

DE KROON (Rembrandtsplein)
Expansive, second-floor Vienna-like gem; an absolutely essential stop.

KAFE VERKEERN (Brouwersgracht 139)
Charming spot slightly off the beaten path, but worth a look-see.

LE MONDE (Rembrandtsplein 6)
>An Amsterdam tradition with heavy gay crowd. Watch the world go by!

OPERA (Rembrandtsplein)
>Acceptable, upscale alternative to De Kroon, if rather less atmospheric. Nice on sunny days, though.

SHOPPING

Amsterdam isn't Paris or Milan; you don't go there to shop.

Yet, while the city is hardly a center of international fashion design, there are more than a few diversions for the shopaholic. While the upscale street of note, P. C. Hoofstraat, is predictable and staid, the boho holes-in-the-wall of the Jordaan are funky and fun—certainly worth an afternoon's rambling.

Highly recommended, too, are the weekend flea markets (see below), full of cultural artifacts and cute men. What more could a shop-till-you-dropper want?

P. C. HOOFSTRAAT and adjoining VAN BAERLE-
>STRAAT (in the vicinity of the museums) are Amsterdam's most chichi shopping streets, offering international designers and Dutch talent both. Rather stuffy—and thus uninteresting—but worth a quick run-through nonetheless.

ROKIN, the canalside thoroughfare, offers upmarket shops, including my personal fave rave, agnès b. (where I found prices lower than in New York and the same as in Paris).

KALVERSTRAAT (from Dan to the Munt) is a curvy, busy consumer's paradise with youth-oriented shops in the mid-price range. Not to be missed: Sissyboy, whose great name is matched by cool duds inside. (Really cute staff, too!)

JORDAAN Lively, formerly working-class (now bohos and yuppies) district is much fun to see by foot, and boasts fab new and used clothing shops, plus the coolest hairdressers in town. A must.

WATERLOOPLEIN The biggest flea market in Holland, a gay destination except Sundays. Books, records, furniture, bric-a-bracs *plus* many cute boys.

MAGNA PLAZA (Nieuwe Zÿds Voorburgwal 182) Eeek! Malls have come to Amsterdam! This one is classy and new, with upmarket shops. Still . . .

GAY

Since Amsterdam's gay scene clusters in four main areas, establishments are listed by neighborhood. In general, Regulierdwarstraat is trendy and young; Warmoesstraat is leatheresque; Kerkstraat falls somewhat nondescriptly in between; and Amstel is famous for its sing-along and hustler bars. Note also that while Amsterdam seems to have a bewildering array of gay bars, there are—depending on your scene—only a few, at any given time, you'll really want to know. That said . . .

REGULIERDWARSTRAAT

CAFÉS

DOWNTOWN (Regulierdwarstraat 31)
    Super-popular gay coffeehouse, popular every day till 8:00 P.M. A must!

OTHER SIDE (Regulierdwarstraat 6)
    Plays second banana to Downtown, but still worth a visit, especially in early evenings.

BACKSTAGE (Utrechsedwarstraat 67)
    Friendly, casual gay café.

BARS

APRIL (Regulierdwarstraat 37)
    An Amsterdam tradition. Young, simpatico, trendy crowd, busy every night. Excellent, cheap draft beer, music videos.

Dance Clubs

EXIT (Regulierdwarstraat 42)
> Crowded, three-story disco palace with youngish clientele. Entry always free. Amsterdam's most-packed gay dance club.

HAVANA (Regulierdwarstraat 17–19)
> Hot new bar/disco complex, packed nightly. Bar-boys are delicious . . .

ROXY (Singel 465)
> Groovy dance club in former cinema. Wednesday is ipso facto gay night, but boys are always welcomed by the postpunk clientele.

Gay-Kerkstraat

Bars

COSMO BAR (Kerkstraat 42)
> Best very late at night. Everybody and anybody.

MEIA MEIA (Kerkstraat 63)
> OK bar. Sunday brunch, if you must.

SPYKER (Kerkstraat 4)
> Leather/Levi's bar cum backroom.

TAVEERNE DE PUL (Kerkstraat 45)
 Traditional Dutch tavern, older clientele.

GAY-WARMOESSTRAAT

BARS

ARGOS (Warmoesstraat 95)
 Leather men at play. Dark room.

CLUB JAECQUES (Warmoesstraat 93)
 Small leather bar, also with playroom. Open early
 evenings.

COCKRING (Warmoesstraat 96)
 Neighborhood's least leather-centered watering
 hole. Disco, backroom, sometimes cute young
 things.

EAGLE (Warmoesstraat 86).
 Need you ask?

G-FORCE (Oudezjids Armsteeg 7)
 S&M. May the force be with you.

STABLEMASTER (Warmoesstraat 23)
 Leather bar with horsey motif.

THE WEB (St. Jacobsstraat 6)
 Reasonable choice for non-leatherettes. Backroom, 'natch.

GAY-AMSTEL

BARS

AMSTEL TAVEERNE (Amstel 54)
Dutch version of a piano bar. Earsplitting sing-along.

COMPANY (Amstel 106)
Mixed, but with a tepid leather influence. Nothin' special.

CUPIDO BAR (Paarderstraat 7)
Trash for cash.

FESTIVAL BAR (Paarderstraat 15)
Ditto.

GAIETY (Amstel 14)
Untrendy, working-class drinking bar.

DANCE CLUBS

IT (Amstelstraat 24)
A must-do Saturday nights: ultra-trendy dance madness. Gay-friendly other nights.

OZON SWING CLUB (Wagenstraat 5)
Dance club. Just OK.

And absolutely do not forget:

TRUT (Bilderdijkstraat 165)
Hyper-trendy dance club, Sunday nights (after midnight) only. East Village-y, very groovy clientele.

SAUNAS

Thermos Day Sauna (Raamstraat 33)
Thermos Night Sauna (Kerkstraat 58)

GAY "CINEMAS"

ADONIS (Warmoesstraat 92)
B-1 (Reguliersbreestraat, 4)
BLUE BOY CLUB (Nieuwezijds Voorburgwal 28)

PORTUGAL

Lisbon

The thing about Lisbon is that it's not like anywhere else.

An elliptical statement, I know, so hear me out. First off, though it's a member of the EEC, Portugal is still a developing country—a fact that pervades every aspect of its daily life. For me, the surest measure of Third World status is a look in the shops: In Lisbon, you just won't find the glitz of Western Europe's best. Nor will you find neon restaurants and cafés; instead, expect local color and—a term I use somewhat euphemistically—"Old World Charm."

Therein, of course, lies Lisbon's appeal. Because it hasn't been tainted by the kind of universal fashion aesthetic that somehow makes world-class cities all feel oddly the same, you'll know you're in a special place. An outpost, maybe; a backwater, perhaps—but an awfully attractive one at that.

Of course, there's an added bonus here: Things in Lisbon are really cheap. Expect to pay far less for a first-class hotel than you would in Paris or Rome; restaurants, too, are less dear. In fact, it's not too much to say that Lisbon remains Europe's last real travel bargain—and who can argue with that?

Lisbon's downtown is fairly compact, perfect for sightseeing on foot. Its undeniable centerpiece is the

Bairro Alto, the oldest part of Lisbon, and a neighborhood whose steep, winding streets haven't changed much in a couple of centuries. It's also the focal point of much of the city's restaurant and nightlife scene—as romantic a part of Europe as you'll ever find.

Romance is much in evidence in the fado, the most easily recognizable Portuguese art form. These slow, sometimes lugubrious folk songs embrace the Porto-Brazilian concept of *saudade* (literally, "sadness," but really, much, much more—*Weltschmerz* is a much better definition of the word). No visit to Lisbon would be complete without an evening spent at one of the Bairro Alto's many traditional fado houses. You may not be able to understand the words, but the feeling of these gorgeous ballads will find its way to your heart.

So, if you're lucky, will the Portuguese men, who are cute, charming, and often uncorrupted by big-city cynicism and cabal. Trust me on this one: Portuguese men have very big hearts and very deep souls, and falling in love with one is a very special treat.

Lisbon's gay nightlife is no dizzying whirl, but it's more than adequate for a city of its size. Most of the clubs are within a stone's throw of one another in the Bairro Alto, making a night on the town a fairly concentrated affair—and hopefully one to remember.

One thing's certain: Charmed by the Portuguese people, the city's sights, and the budget-friendly prices, no one can visit Lisbon just once.

HOTELS

RITZ (Rua Rodrigo da Fonseca, 88; 692020) Lisbon's grande dame, every bit as opulent as you'd expect—and not as pricey as the Ritz in other towns. EXPENSIVE.

DIPLOMATICO (Rua Castilho, 74; 562041) One of Lisbon's best business hotels, with all modern conveniences and a great location. EXPENSIVE.

LISBOA PLAZA (Travessa do Salitre, 7; 3463922) Very elegant hotel right off the main drag; one of the premier addresses in town. EXPENSIVE.

PRINCIPE REAL (Rua de Alegria, 53; 360136) Old World hotel that's very central and very charming with a top-story restaurant boasting an excellent view. Recommended. MODERATE.

INSULANA (Rua Assuncão, 52; 3423131) Small, pension-type hotel that's very central and a winner for the price. INXPENSIVE.

LIS HOTEL (Avenida da Liberdade, 180; 563434) Right on the main boulevard; no beauty, but more than acceptable and as cheap as they come. INEXPENSIVE.

PENSÃO NINHO D'AGUIAS (Costa do Cástelo, 74; 86 70 00) Models, musicians, and young'uns adore this funky little place. INEXPENSIVE.

RESTAURANTS

ATE'LA'IA (Rua da Atalaia 176)
Very "in" Portuguese restaurant with country feel. Lovely.

BARALTO (Rua Diário de Noticias, 31)
Super-cheap, abundant *bonne femme* Portuguese fare. $7 gets you a huge repast.

BOTA ALTA (Travessa da Queimada 35)
Small, animated Bairro Alto institution with a very Lisbon feel. A must!

CASANOSTRA (Travessa do Poco da Cidade, 60)
Bairro Alto Italian eatery frequented by gays. Best Italian food in Lisbon.

CLARA (Campo dos Martires de Patria, 49)
Gorgeous garden restaurant, quite romantic. Portuguese and Continental specialties.

CONVENTUAL (Praça des Flores, 44)
A treat. Recipes come from the monasteries of seventeenth-century Portugal; the result is dishes you won't see anywhere else. Excellent.

ESCORIAL (Rua das Portas de Santo Antão, 47)
Jet-setty crowd, Spanish cuisine. Not cheap, but trendy and very good. Recommended.

GAMBRINUS (Rua das Portas de Santo Antão, 25)
Not a chicspot, but a fabulous place for fish, Portuguese-style.

PAP'AÇORDA (Rua da Atalaia 57)
Very trendy Portuguese restaurant in the Bairro Alto; heavy gay clientele. Fagulous!

TAGIDE (Academia National de Belas Artes, 18)
One of Lisbon's most respected restaurants, with upscale Portuguese/Continental cuisine. A splurge.

XICO CARREIRA (Parque Mayer)
Really cheap, really good, full of local color. Very popular.

SHOPPING

When it comes to shopping in Lisbon, the feel is definitely Third World. The city simply doesn't offer the range of shops—for clothing, at least—that you'd expect to find in an international city of its size.

Since fashion isn't why you come to Lisbon anyway, this shouldn't deter you from the focus of your trip. However, if the urge to shop can't be quelled, know that the city's main shopping area is the Baixa;

the Rua Augusta is the primary artery here. Another modeway is the Rua do Carmo, in the part of the Baixa called Chiado.

The only really compelling thing I find to buy, fashionwise, in Lisbon is shoes. Not groovy platforms or anything like that, but basic, upmarket names like Charles Jourdan and Bally—because of the exchange rate, they tend to be cheaper than in Paris or New York. (Cynic that I am, I tend to think they're not the same quality, either, but—hey—you pays your money, you takes your chances.)

GAY

BARS

BAR 106 (Rua de São Marcal, 106)
> New bar that looks to be a hit; a good place to start early in the evening (after 9:00 P.M.).

FINALMENTE (Rua de Palmeira, 38)
> Drag heaven; the shows are as tacky as you think. Best to go late.

HARRY'S BAR (Rua São Pedro de Alcantara, 57–61)
> Not a gay bar per se; rather, it's the kind of late-night (after 2:00 A.M.) joint where all sorts of night trash (including hustlers) congregate. You decide.

XEQUE-MATE (Rua São Marcal, 170)
> Rather sordid little *boîte;* mucho rough trade.

ALCANTARA-MAR (Rua da Cozinha Economica, 11)
Turn the beat around. Classic disco with mixed gay/straight crowd; not as chic as it once was, but perhaps worth a look-see.

BRICA-A-BAR (Rua Cecilio de Sousa, 84)
Gay dance club with cute young crowd.

FRAGIL (Rua da Atalaia, 128)
Trendy, mixed dance club with (somewhat) groovy young crowd.

TRUMPS (Rua da Imprensa Nacional, 104B)
Mixed, but heavily gay dance spot that's always popular. Worth a trip.

SAUNAS

SAUNA ESTRELA (Avenida Infante Santa, 361, 1st floor)
SAUNA GRECUS (Rua da Telhal, 77, 4th floor)
SPARTACUS (Largo Trinidade Coelho, 2)

SPAIN

Barcelona

How glorious is Barcelona?

Let me put it to you this way: after Paris, it's the European city in which fabulous people say they'd most like to live.

And with good reason: Barcelona is a city whose praises can't be sung highly enough. Equal parts Europe and Spain, "uptown" and "downtown," classical and avant-grade, Barcelona is on every aesthete's A-list of the most spellbinding places in the world.

Imagine, if you will, the tree-lined streets of Paris's best *quartiers*—broad avenues of boundless appeal. That's uptown. Then picture a centuries-old neighborhood of miniscule, winding streets full of rogues, artists, and bohos galore. That's the Barri Gotic, or downtown. Connecting the two is the city's main north-south artery, the Rambla de Catalunya, which turns into the tony Passeig de Gràcia farther uptown.

Some cities grow on you, their attraction not immediately apparent to the untrained eye. Not Barcelona! Show me the man, woman, or child who's not instantly enthralled, and I'll show you someone who's made out of stone.

While always a touristic paradise, Barcelona has only in the past twenty years regained its former esprit de corps. During the repressive regime of Generalissimo Franco, Barcelona's Catalan heritage was squelched; merely speaking the language (don't dare call it a dialect of Castilian Spanish!) was subject to persecution, fines and—quixotically—imprisonment. But no more; today, there's a palpable resurgence of Catalan culture (along, of course, with the popular arts) that helps make Barcelona one of the hottest, hippest cities in Europe.

For most of the eighties, Barcelona was *the* place to be in Spain (Almodovar and his crew of Madrid madcaps notwithstanding); now, in the nineties, the capital is fighting back. The rivalry is friendly, of course; despite high unemployment and the kind of economic problems that plague everywhere, Spain has emerged as a major industrial and cultural force.

To use an American analogy: Madrid is New York, the country's communications and financial capital; Barcelona is San Francisco, all physical beauty, bohemia, and (to detractors) "backwater" allure. Spain fanatics (and who isn't one?) love to debate the two cities' respective merits; I'll let you discover them yourself, for they are many indeed.

After you've spent your days exploring Barcelona's myriad tourist treasures—Gaudí everywhere, the best Picasso museum in the world, fabulous shopping, the atmospheric old port—settle in for a nice, long nap. Dinner in Spain is super-late, often around 10:00 P.M. (though foreigners are given some leeway here!), nightlife a mere whisper before 1:00 A.M. (Exceptions to this rule are the bar/cafés listed below.) But it's all worth waiting for: Barcelona after dark is a decadent, dizzying whirl. The boys are beautiful, the music marvy, and the nights never end. Like everything else about Barcelona, it's the stuff of which the best dreams are made.

HOTELS

CONDES DE BARCELONA (Passeig de Gràcia, 75; 487-3737) Gorgeous old exterior and lobby, totally modern rooms. Excellent "uptown" location, too. VERY EXPENSIVE.

RITZ (Gran Vía, 668; 318-5200) Barcelona's most fashionable address, with all the grandness you'd expect from a Ritz. Fabulous! VERY EXPENSIVE.

CALDERON (Rambla de Catalunya, 26; 301-0000) For travelers who want all the latest conveniences, this hotel is it. Perfect location between up- and downtown. VERY EXPENSIVE.

REGENTE (Rambla de Catalunya, 76; 215-2570) Small "boutique hotel" that's loaded with charm, right on the city's main drag. EXPENSIVE.

GRAN HOTEL HAVANA (Gran Vía, 647; 412-1115) Antique exterior, modern interior; updated luxury here. EXPENSIVE.

ESPAÑA (Sant Pau 9–11; 318-1758) Old hotel that's been updated with excellent results. Absolutely breathtaking Art Nouveau dining rooms. MODERATE.

GRAN VÍA (Gran Vía, 642; 318-1900) Lovely old palace with modernized rooms, yet retaining an Old World feel. Splendid. MODERATE.

ORIENTE (La Rambla, 45–47) An old liberty style gem right on the Rambla. Very atmospheric. MODERATE.

RIALTO (Carrer de Ferrar, 42; 318-5212) An excellent oldster in the Gothic quarter; *muy español.* Recommended. MODERATE.

CIUDAD CONDAL (Carrer de Mallorca, 255; 487-0459) Fine, basic pension with excellent midtown location. INEXPENSIVE.

REIAL (Plaça Real, 11; 302-0366) Hard-core counter-culturists will love this boho dive, right on the Barri Gotic's main square. Less funky types should stay away. INEXPENSIVE.

HOTEL CALIFORNIA (Carrer de Rauric, 14; 317-7766) Very down-and-dirty, very cheap joint in the Gothic quarter that's a stone's throw from the boho bars. Gay-friendly here. INEXPENSIVE.

GAUDI (Carrer Nou de la Rambla, 12; 317-9032) No beauty, but a decent downtown budget spot. INEXPENSIVE.

RESTAURANTS

AGUT (Gignàs, 16)
Lip-smacking Catalan food at impossibly low prices—a perennial Barri Gotic favorite. Recommended.

AGUT D'AVINYÓ (Carrer de la Trinitat, 3)
Excellent Catalan cuisine in a lovely space in the old quarter. Quite charming.

CASA ISIDORE (Carrer de los Flores, 12)
A Catalan classic, around for years—and still one of the locals' favorites. Expensive but worth every cent.

EGIPTE (Carrer de Jerusalem, 3)
A must! Gays, artists, and assorted bohemians have come here for years, and always will—it's the best inexpensive restaurant in town. Just wonderful!

EL GLOP (Carrer de Sant Lluis, 24)
A hearty, unpretentious place with Spanish food for a song. Oh-so-far from chic, but a gourmand's *paradiso*.

LOS CARACOLES (Carrer des Escudellers, 14)
Touristy, sure; but it's also an excellent, fairly cheap place to sample simple Catalan fare. The snails (*caracoles*) are must-haves, of course.

MORDISCO (Carrer del Rossello, 265)
Very "in" place with Nouvelle Catalan fare. Trendoids must not miss it!

NEICHEL (Avenida de Pedralbes, 16)
One of Barcelona's grande dames: updated Catalan cooking at its best. Gastronomes' one big splurge should be this.

NETWORK (Avenida Diagonal, 616)
A bit less chic than several years ago, this super post-modern space is hip, noisy, and must be seen. Gorgeous young Spain at its best.

PASSADIS DEL PER (Plaça de Palau, 2)
A longstanding local favorite, this little place isn't fancy, but offers Catalan cooking with super seafood dishes. For those who love their food and don't need a scene.

QUO VADIS (Carme, 7)
Upscale, "in" restaurant that's considered one of the best in town. Traditional local recipes are king.

SENYOR PARELLADA (Carrer Argentería, 37)
A gorgeous restaurant with fabulous local fare. Unpretentious and excellent.

CAFÉS

CAFÉ DE LA OPERA (Rambla, 74)
Unofficially, *the* gay café on the Rambla, a splendid place to watch the boys—and everyone else—go by. Even cruisy, sometimes.

SHOPPING

The Passeig de Gràcia, upper Rambla, and Avenida Diagonal play home to Barcelona's best shops; the former, especially, merits a nice long look. Don't pass by the indoor, multilevel arcades, the most well known of which is the Bulevar Rosa at Passeig de Gràcia #55.

Scattered among the alleys of the Gothic Quarter are antiques/junk shops, plus a couple of ramshackle outlets where young designers' goods are sold.

GAY

BARS

CAFÉ DE LA CALLE (Carrer Vich, 11)
Interesting bar/café, open from early evening till late.

CAFÉ ROMA (Al Alfons XII)
Sedate new place a bit off the beaten path. Time will tell if it takes off.

ESTEBAR (Carrer Consell de Cent, 257)
Artsy, groovy bar that's definite must-do for the trendoid. Popular from about 11:00 P.M. on.

FLUXUS (Avenida Diagonal, 365)
Cool bar/café with a hippish crowd. Good from 8:00 P.M. on.

GRIS (Carrer Riera de Sant Miguel, 59)
Well-attended drinking bar that's best around midnight. Semi-trendy crowd.

MAN'S (Carrer Valldoncella, 49)
Leather bar.

MONROE'S (Carrer Lincoln, 3)
You guessed it—a Marilyn motif. Semi-trendy young crowd.

PARIS-DAKAR (Carrer San Marcos, 18)
Bar attracting mature crowd, small dance floor.

PUNT (Carrer Muntaner, 63)
Bar/café open from early evening on. Very "in," a must!

ST-GERMAIN DES PRES (Carrer Nueva de San Francisco, 7)
Semi-sleazy; hustlers for days.

SCOTCH 44 (Sant Eusebi, 44)
Older crowd.

XENON (Avenida Meridiana, 140)
Leather crowd reigns here.

DANCE CLUBS

DISTRITO DISINTO (Avenida Meridiana, 140)
Boozy, woozy, floozy disco—a Barcelona late-night institution. Mixed, trendy crowd with heavy gay influence. Opens at 1:00 A.M. but best much later. A must-do for clubbies.

EL CONVENTO (Carrer Bruniguer, 59)
Techno hothouse, cute crowd. Best after 1:00 A.M.

LA LUNA (Avenida Diagonal, 323)
Small, unspectacular disco with backroom. Easy pickups, sometimes.

MARTIN'S (Passeig de Gràcia, 130)
Big, ever-popular disco complex cum upstairs movies and busy backroom. Attracts all kinds of guys, from trendies to average Joes.

METRO (Carrer Sepulveda, 185)
> Large dance club cum backroom. Hot and sweaty—not to be missed.

SANTANASSA (Aribau, 27)
> Sexy young crowd arrives after midnight. Worth a look.

TATU (Carrer Cayo Celio, 7)
> Dancing, shows, backrooms. What a life!

Saunas

BRUC (Carrer Bruc, 65)
CASANOVA (Carrer Casanvova, 57)
CONDAL (Carrer Condal, 18)
PADUA (Carrer La Gleva, 34)
THERMAS (Carrer Diputacion, 46)

Ibiza

Ibiza is to Atlantic City what Paris is to Peoria.

Get the picture? In other words, Ibiza is an absolutely gorgeous island and, despite its intermittent bouts with touristic tackiness, a wonderful place to vacation if you're gay.

Long thought of as an artists' colony, it's no more so today than Greenwich Village is a charming writers' quarter. In Ibiza, everyone rubs shoulders: Germans and Italians, gays and straights, international trendies, and plebs on package tours. The good, the bad, and the ugly all have Ibiza in sight.

Even if you—like me—are no beach bunny, Ibiza's natural beauty and lovely North African–inspired architecture are too enticing to ignore. Besides, it's the perfect adjunct to a trip anywhere else in Spain. Depending on your mood, it can be as relaxing a sunspot or as heady a nightspot as you wish.

But revellers, take note: Anyone wanting to experience the full range of Ibizan madness should make June through August the time to come. Before or after, the crowds are thin; and while, personally, I'd rather hobnob with the boho locals, many of the bars and clubs are closed (or, at the very least, severely underpopulated) off-season. Thus, if you're looking to chill, visit Ibiza whenever; party boys should heed only high season's hedonistic call.

Another caveat: As at most beach resorts, you're a captive customer—and that means expensive restaurants (only a few of which are actually any good) and overpriced bars. However, since hotels are quite reasonable indeed, you shouldn't mind spending a little more in the nightlife category. Besides, for those (*comme moi*) who gain three pounds looking at a leaf of lettuce, food and thongs (or total nudity, acceptable here) don't go together anyway. (Save your bucks and appetite for the gastronomic goodies in the rest of Spain.)

One other thing you need to know: Playa Salinas is the main gay beach, and it's a hike from the lion's share of hotels. In summer, happily, there's a shuttle bus to whisk you to and fro; at other times, you'll have to fend for yourself—and that means a cab ride or an almost prohibitively long walk. More fortuitously, most hotels are an easy stroll from La Puerta, the gay nightlife district in town.

Depending on when you go, Ibiza can be sexy or staid, stagey or sedate. But go you should—it's a destination every gay traveler should "do" at least once.

HOTELS

LA VENTANA (Calle Carroca, 13; 315512) Attractive, popular, small hotel in Old City. MODERATE

HACIENDA NA YAMENA (Partado 423; 333046) The town's luxury address, part of the Relais and Chateaux chain. Gorgeous North African motif, upper crust service; for those who want the best. VERY EXPENSIVE.

ROYAL PLAZA (Calle Pedro Frances, 27; 310000) Nice high-level tourist hotel with all modern conveniences. MODERATE.

EL CORSARIO (Calle Poniente Dalt Vila 5; 301248) Small hotel in town, a good value with some atmosphere. MODERATE.

APARTAHOTEL NAVILA (Plaza Desamparados, 1; 305205) Decent hotel with long-term rates; many gays. MODERATE.

CASA ALEXIO (Barrio Seis Torres, 16; 314249) Small but very nice gay inn that comes highly recommended indeed. MODERATE.

FINCA CANA BLAYA (Centra Cala Llonga, 62; 312129) Old Spanish farmhouse-turned-gay hotel. Not the most central, but a good value and quite unique. MODERATE.

LA MARINA HOTEL (Calle Garijo, 34; 710172) Simple but nice apartment/hotel with many gays. INEXPENSIVE.

RESTAURANTS

CA'N PUJOL (Plaza Port des Torrent)
Fabulous *paella,* cute seaside place. Recommended.

EL GORDON (Strada per S. Eulalia)
Continental cooking; a pretty place with heavy gay clientele.

EL OLIVO (Placa de Vila; 300680)
French eatery with lovely decorations and great food. Very nice.

ESCALAN (Calle Santa Cruz, 6)
German/Continental kitchen that attracts many gays.

FOC I FUM (Calle de la Virgen, 55)
Probably the most popular gay restaurant in Ibiza. Great food and great views. Not to be missed under any circumstances!

S'OFICINA (Avenida de España, 6)
Well-known Basque restaurant in Ibiza's old town. A nice spot indeed.

GAY

BARS

ANGELO (Calle Alfonso XII, 11)
Everybody and anybody comes here; a popular bar with nice terrace. You'll stop in, too.

CATWALK (Calle de la Virgen, 42)
Semi-trendy, less than usually hysterical bar in town. Thus, recommended.

CHIRINGAY (Playa Es Cavallet)
Right on the beach, this is one place you can't avoid. A fun seaside joint, popular during the day.

CRISCO (Calle Ignazio Riquer, 2)
Leather/Levi's bar; dark, trashy, and always busy.

DOME (Calle D'Alfons XII, 5)
Not a gay bar, but international trendies congregate here. A nice respite from all-gay attitude.

GALERIA (Calle de la Virgen, 64)
One of Ibiza's most popular bars, caters to all ages and types. Best around midnight.

INCOGNITO (Calle Santa Lucia, 23)
An absolute must. Perhaps the island's busiest bar, along with Angelo. Cute crowd.

JJ (Calle de la Virgen, 79)
  Butch babes; older, leather-y clientele.

TEATRO (Calle de la Virgen, 83)
  The current favorite among trendoids. Gets going around 11:00 A.M. Fun.

TUBE (Calle Travesia Manuel Sora)
  Another mixed "in" spot with extremely kitschy decor and international crowd. Best to go late.

DANCE CLUBS

ANFORA DISCOTECA (Calle San Carlos, 7)
  Very popular, very crowded dance hall; everyone comes here. Currently riding the techno craze.

SPACE (Playa d'en Bossa)
  Slightly out of town, this place is mixed but has a definite gay presence. It starts going very, very late—well after 4:00 A.M.—and is open on weekends for most of the day. Drugs for days (obviously).

Madrid

Etched indelibly on my mind is the wretched—if requisite—student train ride I took from Paris to Madrid. (Yes, bitch, they *did* have planes in those days, but they were even more frightfully expensive then than they are now.) I'm not sure how long this pilgrimage took, but eighteen hours is the timetable I recall—almost a full day in a hot, cramped, piss-stained "cabin" that surely made my forebears' boat from Europe look like the *QEII*.

The train, it turned out, was the perfect preparation for Madrid—a dusty, dreary backwater that gave the phrase "Old World" new meaning to me. Paris was forward-looking and modern; this place was from the year one, and *everyone* had greasy hair. (Even by 1980, French fags—though not the Gallic population at large—had learned the art of the daily shampoo—*Dieu merci.*) Madrid was more than Old World: it was just plain old.

But that was then, and this is now. Beginning with the eighties' *La Movida* (a movement espousing boundless freedom in society and the arts), the shackles of the decades-long Franco regime loosened. Pedro Almodovar and his band of groovies were at the forefront of this rage. Today Spain—once practically antediluvian—combines its Iberian history with a dizzying whirl of fashion and fantasy, sex and surrealism, artifice and art.

Whereas Barcelona is Europe, Madrid is definitely Spain—in architecture, language, and "feel." There is something tangibly Latin about the city, at once fresh and forward, old and new. Ambling down the Recoletos on a warm summer night, its café terraces bursting with life, you can't help but think you're somewhere terribly important, vital, and fabulously chic.

Madrid's gay scene was, in the eighties, far eclipsed by Barcelona's artsy, flirty days. Today, the city is fighting back hard, and there are not only *muy* cruisy locales, but hyper-trendy clubs as well. The city's night-spots are numerous and naughty, and you'll find all of them profiled here.

Y los hombres? Suffice it to say that if you haven't kissed a Spaniard, you've never been kissed. Go to Madrid, *mis amigos,* have the time of your life, and may you all find the Antonio Banderas of your dreams . . .

HOTELS

RITZ (Plaza de Lealtad, 5; 521-2857) One of Europe's most distinguished hotels—and certainly *numero uno* in Madrid. Impossibly grand and luxurious. *The* place to stay if you can. VERY EXPENSIVE.

PALACE (Plaza de las Cortes, 7; 429-7551) Grand old hotel that's been home to kings, queens (ahem), and celebs galore. Gorgeous lobby, semi-tacky redecorated rooms. VERY EXPENSIVE.

SANTO MAURO (Zurbano, 36; 319-6900) Absolutely gorgeously furnished old mansion with all modern conveniences. A really special place. VERY EXPENSIVE.

REINA VICTORIA (Plaza del Angel, 7; 531-4500) Great old Spanish hotel, recently spruced up. Rather close to gay nightlife, as well. EXPENSIVE.

INGLÉS (Echegaray, 8; 429-6551) Slightly shabby old-ster with artistic/writerly clientele. Very Spanish feel; quite unique. MODERATE.

PARÍS (Alcalá, 2; 521-6496) One of my favorite hotels in Europe. Loads of Castillian charm for a very moderate price. Rooms are big and Spanish in decor; some have balconies that are to die for. Right off the Puerta del Sol, too. MODERATE.

LA MACARENA (Cava de San Miguel, 8; 265-9221) Right off the Plaza Mayor, a great medium-priced hotel residence. Ask for a room with a view. MODERATE.

GALIANO (Calle Miguel Angel, 5; 319-2000) Old house-turned-hotel that's comfortable and central. Nice! MODERATE.

SERRANO (Calle Merques de Villamajor, 8) A charming hotel in a fine part of town, near all of Serrano's shops. A great find for the price. MODERATE.

PRINCIPE PIO (Cuesta de San Vicente, 114; 247-0800) An affordable hotel that's especially popular among Spaniards. MODERATE.

LISBOA (Calle Ventura de la Vega, 17; 429-4676) Everybody's favorite cheap pension-type hotel. You can't beat it for location and price. INEXPENSIVE.

SANTA CRUZ (Plaza Santa Cruz, 6; 522-2441) Another nice pension that's central and cheap. INEXPENSIVE.

MONACO (Barbieri, 5; 522-4630) A fabulously over-the-top place that's close to the Chueca bars. Recommended for budgeteers. INEXPENSIVE.

RESTAURANTS

CAFÉ BALEAR (Sagunto, 18)
> Trendy/fashion types abound; one of Madrid's most "in" dining spots, and a fab place to eat paella.

CAFÉ DE ORIENTE (Plaza de Oriente, 2)
> Incredibly lively multi-room restaurant with different specialties in each (Spanish/French/Continental). Very "in," worth a trip.

CAFÉ GIJÓN (Paseo de Recoletos, 21)
> A Madrid tradition, a restaurant/bar/café that's ostensibly a writer/artist hangout but attracts the

gamut of gays and tony types. Hustlers, too—oddly
enough.

CASA CIRIACO (Plaza Mayor, 84)
An age-old always-popular place to sample Madrid's local fare. Yummy and not too expensive.

EL INGENIO (Calle Leganitos, 10)
Somewhat touristy, but an excellent, inexpensive place to sample typical Castilian fare.

JOCKEY (Calle Almador de los Rios, 6)
A longtime upscale favorite, with recipes from Spain and beyond. A great business/splurge place, *muy elegante.*

LA TRAINERA (Calle Lagasca, 60)
One of Madrid's most well-respected seafood restaurants, with the freshest fish imaginable. Scrumptious!

PINOCHO (Calle Orfila, 2)
Theatrical/movie crowd in chic Italian eatery. Way "in."

SACHA (Calle Juan Hurtado de Mendoza, 11)
Fabulous Continental cuisine, beautiful, hip crowd. Trendies: do not miss!

TABERNA DEL ALBARDERO (Calle Felipe, 6)
Old World charm for days, this *tapas* bar/restau-

rant is inexpensive and high on everyone's list. Not trendy, just local fun.

VIRIDIANA (Calle Juan de Mena, 14)
One of Madrid's most innovative kitchens; chichi crowd. Nice!

ZALACAÍN (Calle Alvarez de Baena, 4)
Many say this is Madrid's finest restaurant—an opulent, super-expensive temple to haute cuisine *française;* a Basque influence, too. The top of the line.

ZARA (Calle Infantas, 5)
Cuban eatery attracting artists, gays, bohos. Lively and very fun.

SHOPPING

Once a sartorial backwater, Spain has captured the attention of the world for its forceful, witty, and very sexy fashion stance. From haute couture to the avant-garde, Madrid has it all.

Fans of design and the graphic arts will absolutely appreciate merchandising in Madrid, which is rather more like the fanciful creations of New York than the staid presentation one finds in Paris these days. Shops are full of fabulous goods and hip, good-looking staff; even a non-consumerist like me can be won over quick.

That said, here's where to go:

ALMIRANTE is Madrid's version of SoHo in New

York—an upscale-yet-downtown shopping district that attracts Spain's hottest young designers. The street runs from Barquillo to Recoletos; don't fail to miss its side arteries, the most important of which is Xiquena.

SALAMANCA is Madrid's Fifth Avenue, home to Spanish designers and international names both. Whereas Almirante is geared toward the super-trendy and avant-garde, Salamanca plays host to established, conservative clothes and "high-fashion" stuff. Again, don't bypass the side streets, all of which contain shops; Serrano is the key avenue here.

GAY

CAFÉS

FIGUEROA (Calle Augusto Figueroa, 17)
> Very popular, and a great place to hang out from afternoon on. Absolutely a must-do!

BARS

BLACK AND WHITE (Calle de la Libertad, 34)
> One of Madrid's oldest gay institutions—an interesting relic, but not much more. Hustlers abound; the small dance floor is usually no man's land.

BUNBURY (Plaza de Chueca, 10)
> Newish bar that a young, semi-trendy crowd frequents after the other bars close (4:00 A.M. or so).

CRUISING (Calle Perz Galdos, 5)
Very busy bar that's hot after midnight; backroom roars. A Madrid institution.

KITARO (Calle Barbiri, 7)
Not a gay bar per se, but home to a trendy young crowd into modern music and styles. Fashion victims take note!

LA BABU (Calle Recoletos, 11)
Piss-elegant place attracting a mature clientele.

LA CUEVA (Calle Villalar, 1)
Old-style bar with dancing, sometimes; fairly working-class Spanish crowd.

LA LUPE (Torrecilla del Leal, 12)
Also not strictly gay, but young alternative trendoids abound. Quite fun, beginning around midnight.

LEATHER BAR (Calle Pelayo, 42)
Guess what? Some non-leather types, too.

LE BILBOUBOQUET (Calle Marques del Duero, 8)
Undistinguished bar catering to older crowd; drag and other shows, sometimes.

LORD BYRON'S (Calle Recoletos, 18)
Slightly pissy bar with upscale clientele. Eleganza!

MADRID LA NUIT (Calle Pealyo, 31)
  Very popular bar for Madrid's mature men.

PLAZA DEL REY (Plaza del Rey)
  Mixed, but with heavy gay influence. Very "in" for fashionites just now.

RICK'S (Calle Clavel, 8)
  Another mixed, trendy joint that's major fun on weekend nights. The best of young Madrid.

RIMMEL (Calle Luis de Gongora, 2)
  One of the best places to go early-ish; cruisy young crowd. A must.

TROYANS (Calle Pelayo, 4)
  Most popular leather bar in town; backroom, too.

VERY, VERY BOYS (Calle de la Libertad, 4)
  Sexy new place with horny young'uns; funroom in back.

DANCE CLUBS

ALES (Calle Veneras, 2)
  One of Madrid's most popular spots for years, and still going strong. All types, including many sexy guys. Very busy backroom, as well.

BACHELOR (Calle Reina, 2)
  Euro-style disco that's hit or miss, but worth a look-see. You never know . . .

DUPLEX (Calle de Hortaleza, 64)
  Perhaps Madrid's most "in" spot for gay trendoids; a must if that's your scene.

EL MOROCCO (Calle Marques de Leganes, 7)
  Another mixed trendspot that boasts Moroccan decor and great dance sounds.

HANOI (Calle Hortaleza, 81)
  Super in-spot for the fashion crowd with definite gay presence. Way cool.

STELLA (Calle Cedaceras, 17)
  Another mixed dance palace for people of the night, most heavily gay on weekends. Very trendy indeed.

SAUNAS

ADAN (Calle San Bernardo, 38)
ALAMEDA (Calle Alameda, 20)
COMENDADORAS (Plaza de la Comendadoras, 9)
INTERNACIONAL I (Calle Olivar, 1)
INTERNACIONAL II (Calle Altamirano, 37)
INTERNACIONAL III (Calle Maestro Arbos, 23)
PARAISO (Calle Norte, 15)

PELAYO (Calle Pelayo, 25)
PLAZA SAUNA (Edificio España in the Galería Comercial)
SAUNA PRINCIPE (Calle Principe, 15)

Sitges

Less than an hour from Barcelona, *très gay* Sitges is a fabulous stopover for nightcrawlers and sun queens alike. The town doesn't even begin to rival Ibiza's setting and charm; what it does have going for it is proximity to Barcelona and a nutsy night scene all its own.

When Ibiza went out of fashion several years ago (it's now back with a vengeance, of course), Sitges sat up and took up the slack. In fact, it has even become chic for Barcelonans to live in Sitges year-round, so easy is the commute and so calming is life on the Spanish beach.

Sitges may have less of an international crowd than Ibiza, but that can be easily construed as a plus. After all, what would *you* rather look at beachside: pasty Britons with bad bods or Hispanic hunks? (OK, OK—I know this sentence is egregious on two fronts: There are some Englishmen with good bodies, and "Hispanic" refers to Spanish speakers in the Americas, not Europe; but what's a travel book without some low-rent alliteration anyway?)

July and August are the big months here, and though the town is crowded, it really is the time to come. Sitges boasts of its museums, but they're actually rather arcane, and its restaurants hardly pose a threat to the best in Spain. No, what you come here for is the sea and the studs—and if the latter aren't around, why bother to come at all?

For summer travelers to Barcelona, a layover in sexy Sitges—smutty pun intended!—can be a hot ticket indeed.

HOTELS

CALIPOLIS (Passeig Maritim; 894-1500) Somewhat characterless and overpriced quasi-modern hotel, but popular for its location and conveniences. EXPENSIVE.

MADISON (Carrer San Bartolome, 9; 894-6147) Decent pension-type hotel with visible gay clientele. Fine, really. MODERATE.

HOTEL DE LA RENAIXENCA (Carrer Isla de Cuba, 13) Very nice hotel, practically all gay, and a perennial favorite. MODERATE.

ROMANTIC HOTEL (Carrer de Sant Isidre, 33) Absolutely charming; the best place in town to stay. Gorgeous old villa that international gays adore. MODERATE.

Note: There are also several apartment-type residences, excellent for longer stays, that can be reserved through the German group Mantours. In the U.S., you can book through gay travel agencies (which advertise in all the gay newspapers and magazines).

RESTAURANTS

CASA HIDALGO (San Pablo, 12)
Spanish cooking at its best. Popular among gays and straights alike.

CELLER DEL BON VI (Carrer de la Carreta, 21)
Wonderful, casual Catalan cooking; definite gay clientele.

CHEZ NOUS (Passeig Vilafranca, 2)
Swiss kitchen, gay crowd. Very popular.

EL TRULL (Carrer M. Felix Clara, 3)
Somewhat expensive French restaurant that's popular among visiting gays.

FLAMBOYANT (Carrer Pablo Barrabeig, 6)
Piss-elegant place that's overpriced but a nice place for a date.

MA MAISON (Carrer Bonaire, 28)
French and Continental kitchen attracts hungry tourists, gay and straight. Nice.

PICNIC (Passeig del Mar at Avenida Fernandez)
Casual place near the beach with semi-gay clientele.

CAFÉS

ELSA (Carrer Parelladas, 86)
Cute café with heavy gay crowd. Good days.

GOYA (Carrer San Francisco, 42)
Not totally gay, but a friendly, casual place, especially early evenings.

GAY

BARS

BOURBON'S (Carrer San Buenaventura, 13)
Bar/disco that attracts a hip, good-looking crowd. A must!

EL CANDIL (Carrer de la Carreta, 9)
All kinds of guys congregate in this Euroclub. Bar, small disco, etc.

EL HORNO (Carrer Juan Tarrida Ferratyes, 6)
Sitges's most popular leather bar.

EL PUCHERO (Carrer San Jose, 22)
Small bar with varied clientele; hit or miss.

EL 7 (Carrer Nueva, 7)
Amiable bar cum backroom that gets started earlier than most. Worth a try.

LORD'S (Carrer Marques de Montroig, 16)
Just OK bar/disco for older crowd.

PARROT'S PUB (Plaza Industria, 2)
Decent watering hole that is best in early evening; all types come here.

REFLEJOS (Carrer San Buenaventura, 19)
Trendy, mixed bar that's one of the hippest spots in town.

Dance Clubs

MEDITERRANEO (Carrer San Buenaventura, 6)
Incredibly popular dance palace, great international dance sounds. A little seventies, but who cares?

TRAILER (Carrer Angel Vidal, 36)
The club of the moment—all the sexy boys are here. Goes until very late at night indeed. Not to be missed!

Sauna

SAUNA SITGES (Carrer Espalter, 11)

SWITZERLAND

Bern

Blessed with a unified architecture—a breathless maze of arcaded passageways—Bern is Switzerland's Bologna, possessed of a magic found in few cities on Earth.

You might imagine the political capital of the world's most retentive nation to have a bug up its ass; such is most assuredly not the case. Now, I'm not suggesting you spend a week here, but Bern does hold the promise of an awfully nice day.

The city has a good art museum, several memorable restaurants, and one great café, the Diagonal. But none of this is the name of Bern's tourism game; shopping is. In the way that Florence's fabulous shops are inseparable from their architectural housings, so are Bern's: You really know you're in Europe here.

There are some cute clothing stores, but nothing to touch what you'd find in the major cities of the world. What you'll find are ultra-modern design showcases offering the latest in accessories, furniture, and bric-a-brac. The prices slant sky-high, but window-shopping makes a fine day's sport.

Bern's gay nightlife is hardly spectacular, but is most certainly respectable for a city of its size (and for those so inclined, there are always the baths). This little jewel of a city is probably nowhere you've given much thought to going—though for its homespun allure, when en route to Geneva or Zurich, you probably should.

HOTELS

BELLEVUE PALACE (Kochergasse 3; 320-45-45) Bern's priciest, most elegant hotel; Old World charm for days, rooms with panoramic city views. VERY EXPEN-SIVE.

BELLE EPOQUE (Gerechtigkeitsgasse 18; 311-43-36) Art Nouveau showplace, just this side of stuffy. The bar is a scene in itself. EXPENSIVE.

GOLDENER ADLER (Gerechtigkeitsgasse 7; 311-17-25) Small, centrally located gem in former private home; good Swiss restaurant on site. MODERATE.

GLOCKE (Rathausgasse 75; 311-37-71) Basic, yet most acceptable place to stay, right in the center of town. Swiss and Italian eateries here. INEXPENSIVE.

GOLDENER SCHLUESSEL (Rathausgasse 72; 311-02-16) Another bargain, very central. Iffy Mexican cuisine best avoided, amigos. INEXPENSIVE.

RESTAURANTS

BELLEVUE GRILL (Kochergasse 3)
Ostensibly, Bern's poshest dining room, with classic Continental cuisine. For those who can splurge.

DELLA CASA (Schauplatzgasse 16)
Italian cooking meets Swiss-German cuisine, with stunning results.

HARMONIE (Hotelgasse 3)
Totally unpretentious, a great place to sample the hearty local fare for a song.

LORENZINI (Marktgass-Passage 3)
Bern's major "trendy" restaurant; tremendous Northern Italian kitchen. The bar, though very hetero, is a scene.

THAI FOOD KURIER (Gerechtigkeitsgasse 9)
Popular among groovy young Berners.

ZUM RATHAUS (Rathausplatz 5)
A local favorite, heavy on woodsy decor—and on the stomach, as Swiss is the order of the day.

SHOPPING

Bern is not huge, and a couple of hours is enough to traverse its lovely arcaded pedestrian streets. The ones not to miss: Spitalgasse, Marktgasse, Kramgasse, Postgasse, and Gerechtigkeitsgasse. Globus (Spitalgasse 17) is the major department store.

GAY

BARS AND CLUBS

BABA LU ACTION (Gurtengasse 3)
Dance club for trendy, mixed clientele; Wednesdays only.

URSUS CLUB (Junkernstrasse 1)
Standard-issue bar/disco, the only ongoing place in town. Slants youngward.

SAUNAS

AL PETER'S SUN DECK (Lauegass Strasse 65)
STUDIO 43 (Monbijoustrasse 123)

Geneva

German-speaking Switzerland: placid and dull. French-speaking: fun, fun, fun. Seems like a reasonable assumption, no?

No! While Zurich is a city that sparkles, Geneva—sorry, guys—is Dullsville all the way.

Maybe it's the heaviness of the city's venerable institutions—the Red Cross, League of Nations, etc.—that imparts such a solemn air. Or maybe it's the oft-spoken sentiment that the French Swiss wallow in a permanent inferiority complex (as in, "They're not *really* French"). Whatever the reason, Geneva just isn't on a par with Europe's best.

That said, I'm of the opinion that any place is worth visiting at least once, so travelers in this neck of the woods may find a brief visit worth their while. Perhaps even more likely is that you'll find yourself here on business; Geneva is, of course, one of the great financial centers of the world.

On the surface, Geneva is a kind of Paris manqué: It's got the river and bridges, though both are rather less spectacular than those in the City of Lights. And there are a handful of decent museums and one great one (devoted to the activities of the International Red Cross—a hugely moving "must-see").

So, at least superficially, Geneva has all the makings of a top-flight tourist town. Yet something's missing.

Geneva displays a curious lack of energy, a certain *je ne sais quoi* that just isn't there—a fact all but die-hard locals will readily admit. Unlike Zurich, which boasts around-the-clock throngs, Geneva's street life is a relatively sad affair. This is due, at least partly, to the lack of discernible *grands boulevards;* but it's probably even more a reflection of the city's basic character—serious, conservative, *comme il faut.* (The obvious exceptions are the gently winding streets of the Old City, a nice place to stroll on warm summer eves.)

Nightlife? Don't make me laugh! First, the prohibitive cost of restaurants makes dining out a rare treat for all but the businessman and well-to-do. There's nothing even vaguely like New York's East Village, no pocket of ethnic shitholes where you can eat for seven bucks. Clubs, too, are expensive, which means that, even for young'uns in the richest country in the world (Switzerland's per capita income is number one), "going out" is hardly an every-night affair. The bottom line: For all intents and purposes, Genevans are pretty much "in for the night" all the time.

Gay life exists, though with the same sense of inertia as things in general here. Weekdays are almost universally dull, and the saunas see more action than the bars. The Swiss reputation for being no nonsense is certainly well-deserved. On weekends, things pick up a little, especially at the Déclic and Musicol. (Major party queens may want to check out the scene in Lausanne, a half hour away, which boasts impromptu "raves," especially during summertime. Posters in the bars cited below will tell you when and where.)

The bottom line: You'll not want to make Geneva your dream destination, but as a two-day trifle, it's an acceptable pit stop.

HOTELS

HOTEL DU RHÔNE (1, quai Turrettini; 731 98 31) This five-star hotel's list of celebrity guests will make you dizzy. And deservedly so: The hotel's riverfront location, famed eating spots, and excellent staff make the Rhône a terribly correct choice. VERY EXPENSIVE.

BEAU RIVAGE (13, quai du Mont-Blanc; 731 02 21) Geneva's grande dame, an old, elegant jewel right on the Rhône. Terribly, terribly grand—and *cher*. VERY EXPENSIVE.

D'ALLEVES (13, rue Kleberg; 738 32 66) Best bet for the price: central location of Victorian charm for days. MODERATE.

STRASBOURG-UNIVERS (10, rue Jean-Jacques Pradie; 732 25 62) Another good, moderately priced choice, recently renovated and close to gay scene. MODERATE.

CENTRAL (2, rue de la Rôtisserie; 31 45 94) Pension-type lodging: no frills, but clean, central, and cheap. INEXPENSIVE.

DE LA CLOCHE (6, rue de la Cloche; 732 94 81) Another pension-type choice. Drawback: no private baths. Plus: great option for the price. You decide. INEXPENSIVE.

BEAU SITE (3, place du Cirque; 328 10 08) For the price, a fair degree of charm. Recommended. INEXPENSIVE.

RESTAURANTS

BAR DE COUTANCE (16, rue de Coutance)
Family-run Italian eatery, also featuring French-Swiss specialties. Moderately priced.

BOEUF ROUGE (7, rue de Paquis)
Unpretentious little restaurant, a great place to sample local color and fare. Highly recommended.

CAFÉ DU GRUETLI (16, rue General-Dufour)
Groovy crowd, hip decor. Light, popularly priced, fare. A trendie's must-do.

CAFÉ DU VALLON (182, rue de Florissant)
Lively, casual bistro in close-in residential quarter. Untouristy, authentic spot. Recommended.

LA CASSOLETTE (31, rue Jacques Dalphin)
A favorite among Geneva's "in" crowd (such as

they are): innovative cooking in the charming Car-
ouge area.

LA FAVOLA (15, rue Jean-Calvin)
Updated classic Italian, one of the most popular
spots in town.

L'ESCALADE (8, rue de Coutance)
A real Genevan spot: cozy, woodsy atmosphere;
great omelettes, croques, and the like. Cute!

L'EVIDENCE (13, rue des Grottes)
Rather gay restaurant cum piano bar. A good
place to get acquainted with the local scene.

LE CYGNE (in Hilton Hotel, 19, quai du Mont-Blanc)
Probably the city's most well-known restaurant,
featuring a renowned nouvelle chef and fabulous
river views. Ungodly expensive.

NEPTUNE (in Hotel du Rhône, quai Turrettini 1)
The city's newest rising star. Former Le Cygne
chef now weaves magic in exclusive, mainly fishy,
spot. Frightfully expensive, but oh-so-chic.

ROBERTO (10, rue Pierre Fatio)
Arguably the best Italian spot in town. Fabulous,
but not cheap.

SHOPPING

Truth be told, Geneva's reputation as a shopper's Eden is utterly ill-deserved. As Swiss cities go, both Bern and Zurich have altogether more interesting places to shop. Yes, the rue du Rhône hosts all the big guns—Lanvin, Chanel, et al.—but who, apart from oil sheiks, really buys that stuff? If constipated "designers" are your bag, you're in luck, but there's shockingly little of contemporary appeal.

That said, you should plan to spend a couple of hours on the rue du Rhône and its environs (rue du Marché, rue de la Croix-d'Or) to get a taste of Genevan life. Far more interesting is the Old Town area that surrounds the charming place du Bourg-de-Four (somewhat reminiscent of Paris's Place du Tertre in Montmartre). Here, you'll find a smattering of *antiquaires,* bookstores, art galleries, and other artsy boutiques.

Confirmed mall addicts can while away an hour at the glass-and-chrome (read: dated) Centre-Confédération that sits off the rue du Rhône. Those committed to department stores can amble around the Grand Passage (rue du Rhône 50) or Bon Génie (rue de Marché 34), though both are mid-market and of less than penetrating interest. In sum, saving your money will be easy to do here.

GAY

BARS

CONCORDE (3, rue de Berne)
Trash for cash. *Capisce?*

LA CHAUMETTE (11, rue des Etuves)
Friendly little watering hole, best in early evenings.
Multilingual musical acts, at times.

LA GARCONNIERE (22, place Bémont)
All ages, mixed bag. Best from 10 P.M. on.

LE DECLIC (28, boulevard du Pont d'Arve)
Perhaps Geneva's most popular bar; all ages,
though slants young.

LE KID (7, rue Leschot)
Mixed, druggy late-night spot that *opens* at 4 A.M.
You can imagine what you'll find . . .

L'HIPPOCAMPE (47, rue Pâquis)
Tiny, shiny, tacky bar. On weekends, if you're in
the nabe.

LE TUBE (3, rue de l'Université)
Best bet for young crowd. After work and onwards,
though best around midnight.

Dance Club

LE MUSICOL (5, rue Richemont)
> Bad drag shows, strippers sometimes. Hodge-
> podge, but the only real gay disco in town. (And
> *not* cheap!)

Saunas

BAINS DE L'EST (3, rue de L'est)
GEM AUX SAUNA (4, rue Prévost-Martin)
PRADIER SAUNA (8, rue Pradier)

Zurich

Pretty, cozy, and easy to get to know, Zurich fits like a warm old glove. What it lacks in New York's frenzy or Paris's nonstop allure, the city more than makes up for in quiet charm; though not an ultimate destination, it's a lovely stopover for a couple of days.

How you feel about Zurich depends, of course, on your inclination—or aversion—to Germanic culture as a whole, and I'll not try to convince Teutonophobes that they're likely to love Zurich if they hate Hamburg or Berlin. Still, the town should prove of more than mild interest to the Swissaholic and general visitor both.

If pressed, one could "do" Zurich in a day: a hike down the Bahnhofstrasse, across the Quai Bruecke, then around trendy Niederdorf, and you've pretty much done the Zurich thang. There's a good (not great) art gallery, the Kunsthaus, and the Swiss National Museum (of interest to devotees of local history and hard-core Heidi nuts). Throw in the Opera House and a church or two, and you can stretch your visit to a second day. Else, one day'll do ya, and you can move on to greener pastures in Switzerland or beyond.

Gay life in Zurich is open, if not excessively lively: one disco, a few sedate bars, and a good stock of saunas sums up the scene. Serious clubhounds should check out *Cruiser,* the local gay newspaper, for info on traveling clubs and other special nightlife events.

HOTELS

BAUR AU LAC (Talstrasse 1; 221-16-50) Zurich's grand dame, right off the picturesque Zurichsee. Discreet, old-money feel. VERY EXPENSIVE.

DOLDER GRAND (Kurhausstrasse 65; 251-62-31) More than grand—a fucking fortress reached best by funicular tram. Not super-central, but as posh as they come. Its heralded restaurant is haute cuisine at its best. VERY EXPENSIVE.

ZUM STORCHEN (Weinplatz 2; 211-55-10) Very central, very correct. Rooms with river view are to die for! EXPENSIVE.

ROESSLI (Roessligasse 7; 252-2121) Zurich's answer to New York's Paramount Hotel: post-modern decor, super-trendy crowd. The ne plus ultra of international hip. MODERATE.

WELLENBERG (Niederdorfstrasse 10; 262-43-00) A poor man's Roessli: heavy on the late-seventies black lacquer look, but a great location makes this a reasonable choice. MODERATE.

LIMMATHOF (Limmatquai 142; 261-42-20) Zurich's best budget option, a stone's throw from the main train station and right off the Niederdorfstrasse. Clean, tiny rooms, helpful desk staff. INEXPENSIVE.

RESTAURANTS

In Zurich, as in the rest of Switzerland, the notion of a trendy restaurant is virtually unknown. The following choices are therefore made for their notable local color and cuisine, not their relative chic.

KOENIGSTUHL (Stuessihofstatt 3)
Swiss guild decor gone (intentionally) amuk. A nouvelle cuisine bistro and classic European kitchen both. You decide.

KRONENHALLE (Raemistrasse 4)
Traditionally Germanic, woodsy decor; super-heavy traditional fare. A local legend—a must-do!

MERE CATHERINE (Naeelihof 3)
An informal French bistro with decent price and unstuffy crowd. Nice.

TUEBLI (Scheggengasse 8)
Noted for its irreverent, nouvelle-y menus and experimental cooking styles, this touted gem is for the gastronomically avant-garde.

ZEUGHAUSKELLE (Bahnhofstrasse 28)
A Zurich institution. Beer and bratwurst, noisy and cheap.

ZUNFTHAUS ZUR WAAG (Muensterhof 8)

A basic Guild house, famed for its hefty servings of stick-to-the-ribs Swiss fare.

SHOPPING

The draw here is local curios (clunky, woodsy stuff), chocolate (a must), and watches (make sure they're really cheaper than back home). Buy the latter on the Bahnhofstrasse, Zurich's almost Fifth Avenue, which plays home to the likes of Benetton, midmarket department stores, and—best of all!—an Yves Rocher outpost (for fabulous masks and moisturizers, much cheaper than at home).

Storchengasse houses Zurich's priciest boutiques, including Versace (#23) and Trois Pommes (#6). The latter has a small, but choice, selection of top-notch men's designer goods, offered at reduced prices in their "Checkout" branch (at Toedistrasse 44).

But all of the above pale in comparison to the wares you'll find on Niederdorfstrasse in Old Town, which is where hip young Zurich shops. (Wandering around this funky nabe merits an afternoon anyhow.) Best bet: Relief (Stuessilhafstatt 17 at Limmatquai)— for my money, the coolest store in town.

GAY

BARS

Note: This ain't Madrid; pubs are usually open only till midnight—a nice concept for people with day jobs!

EMILIO'S BAGPIPER (Zaehringerstrasse 11)
Gemuetlich little tavern open from late afternoon on. A cute stopover for hearty local specialties by day; cruisy by night. Zurich's most popular bar.

BLUE BOX BAR (Konradstrasse 13)
Friendly, mixed crowd; excellent jukebox. Fondue, other food, and musical entertainment sometimes. A happy hour favorite.

TIP-TOP (Seilengraben 13)
Nice enough pub, reasonable for a quick stopover. All ages welcome.

DANCE CLUBS

MASCOTTE (Theaterstrasse 10)
A local legend, put on by the boys at Club HEY. Only Sunday is gay, but it's a hot ticket then.

T & M (Marktgasse, 14)
The ongoing gay disco. Acceptable, if hardly a bea-

con of the avant-garde. Open till 4 A.M. on weekends.

SAUNAS

ADONIS (Mutschellenstrasse 17)
APOLLO (Selergraben 14)
CITY (Zentralstrasse 45)
DAVID SAUNA CLUB (Kanzleistrasse 84)
MOUSTCHE RELAX CLUB (Badenerstrasse 156b)
MYLORD (Seebahnstrasse 139)
PARAGON RELAX CLUB (Muehlegasse 11)
RENO'S RELAX CLUB SAUNA (Kernstrasse 57)

About the Author

David Andrusia, a former movie studio executive, is the author of *Europe Hot and Hip*. He has contributed to *Interview, Details, The Advocate, In Fashion,* and many other magazines. Fluent in six languages, he lives in New York City.